THE STANDARD I

The Standard Directory of Proof Marks

WITH WW II GERMAN ORDNANCE CODES

by Gerhard Wirnsberger
translated by R.A. Steindler

Distributed by

800-531-2665

Published by Jolex, Inc.

LC Number: 75-11048

ISBN: 0-89149-006-X

TABLE OF CONTENTS

FOREWORD

On every important part of every shoulder gun or handgun sold in Germany, you will find a small mark. This is the mark of the proof house where the gun underwent proof. The affixing of this mark and the actual proofing of the gun is done under the rules and regulations of the German proof law. Initiated on May 19, 1891, the law in part states:

"The law about official proof of the barrels and locks of handheld guns is designed to stimulate our domestic arms makers and make them more competitive in the export market. The law serves to protect the buying public from unscrupulous manufacturers, and will also affect the existing rules and regulations as they pertain to arms makers and the trade in guns."

From these few lines, the basic concept of the proof law becomes clear. Most of the European countries and many countries overseas have also established proof laws, and most of them are reciprocal: that is, one country accepts the proof standards of the other country. Of course, the basic proof laws vary somewhat, but essentially they are very much alike.

The most important aspect of the proof law is that the hunter and shooter is able to identify the proof marks, especially on older guns. It is important to know if the gun was proofed for nitro or black powder, since the modern propellants deliver much higher chamber pressures than cartridges loaded with black powder. Naturally, the condition of the gun and the functioning of the safety also play a role in buying or selling such a gun.

The chapters of this book have been designed so that each time segment covered by a specific proof law is contained within that chapter, so that establishing the approximate age of a gun is greatly facilitated, providing the proof mark has a time limit.

Since Baron Engelhardt concluded his basic research of proof marks in 1955, it has become essential to update proof laws and include the new regulations. This has sometimes created seemingly contradictory statements in a chapter—statements which are, however, historically and legally correct.

Gerhard Wirnsberger

INTRODUCTION

The development of the proof mark dates back to the 16th century, perhaps even earlier. It is quite conceivable that proof marks date even further back in history, but the marks themselves have remained unknown to researchers and students. The earliest proof marks are sometimes undistinguishable from the master guild mark or the city mark. For instance, the cities of Augsburg and Nürnberg have inspection marks, while Essen and Suhl have real proof marks. In the first instance, the gun was visually inspected, while the city fathers of Essen and Suhl insisted on an actual shooting test before the city's mark was affixed, with the shooting being done with an extra stiff charge or load—the proof load.

This uncertainty about the history of proof marks leaves many unexplored areas for the arms student and historian. The hunter, on the other hand, is concerned primarily with modern proof, wanting to know what the mark on his gun signifies. His interest may extend to grandfather's old rifle or fowling piece. Interest in proof marks may also extend to a shooter who somehow abtained a few old military rifles.

Similarly, the gunsmith must often determine the origin or soundness of a gun, and, with the help of the proof marks, he can readily do both.

I have limited myself here to the currently used proof marks of the various European countries. As of the moment, the United States of America still does not have a proof law, and the proof marks of the various American gun companies are not accepted as proof by the European proof houses. Firearms carrying the proof marks of these American gun makers must undergo proof before they can be sold in Europe. Mention is also made of those guns which are out of proof, but which are still useable and regularly find their way onto the gun market, where recognizing and understanding the proof marks can be of importance to the shooter. Similarly, a few Spanish and French proof marks are included which serve to show the arms student just how long ago this specific gun was made, and that usage of such a gun must be predicated on a thorough examination of the gun by a competent gunsmith. Thanks to proof and allied marks, it sometimes becomes possible to date a gun precisely.

Today's most important role of the proof mark is to show that the gun in question is safe to be fired with smokeless powder charges. The strength of the proof load has been determined by the international agreements of July 14, 1914, and 1924 at the Brussels, Belgium meetings. The countries attending these meetings have, to this day, very similar, if not identical, proof loads. However, the proof load used by the participating countries is also highly specific for the country using it.

For example, international rules call for a second or final proof of a shotgun with black powder, and the load developing 8818 psi (pounds per square inch) must be handled without trouble. For a smokeless propellant, the required pressure limit is 12,089 psi. These pressure levels were, until quite recently, adequate, but since the appearance of the extra powerful cartridges from the United States, the standard had to be revised upwards. Some of this ammunition develops pressure levels equal to that prescribed for proof loads, and shooters and hunters are cautioned about the use of such shells in guns carrying proof marks indicating normal proof loads and therefore normal proof pressures.

In some countries there exists a special proof which calls for a pressure level of 12,800 psi. However, in all of the more progressive rules of proof, the final black powder proof for double-barrel shotguns has been eliminated and each smoothbored gun, for which smokeless powder shells are being sold, must also be proofed for smokeless powder. The British proof law of Augugst 3, 1925 began a trend in that direction. Shortly thereafter, the Czech and the German proof laws of June 7, 1939, were enacted. The German law is recognized the world over as one of the best proof laws. The Austrian rules of proof followed on July 30, 1951.

In the question of cartridges loaded with a bullet, the most widely accepted rule calls for an overload or proof load that creates a pressure level in excess of 30 per cent over the normal chamber pressure. In the case of handgun ammunition, black powder proof calls for a 30 per cent increase in pressure, while cartridges loeded with smokeless powder are permitted a pressure increase of 50 per cent.

AUSTRIA-HUNGARY

Shortly after the German proof law became effective on May 19, 1891, the Austro-Hungarian empire established its first rule of proof on June 23, 1891. The new law became effective as of April 1, 1893 in Germany, and in Austria-Hungary, the first proof rules became law on January 1, 1892. However, the State of Carinthia, in Austria, had its own proof law which had become effective on November 25, 1882. This was a voluntary proof for hand-held guns. The small town of Ferlach—long a gun-making center very much like Suhl, Liege or Eibar—more or less satisfied the demand of the Imperial sovereign states and countries, including the Balkan, for inexpensive rifles.

Space precludes discussion of the Ferlach proof rules, and it must suffice here to say that these rules were patterned after those established for Liege. The proof mark was affixed, after the first proof, to the unifinished barrel. For this proof, black powder was used, and the charge consisted of 2/3 of the weight of the lead ball of the suitable caliber. Thus, a 16 gauge barrel was tested with 277.78 grains (18 grams) of black powder. The second proof was performed with a black powder load reduced 1/3 of the first charge, and was marked on the barrel .

The so-called third proof was designed to show if the barrel survived the first and second proof load, if the proof marks were applied properly, and if closure between barrel and receiver was still tight. Based on an examination and using the above criteria, the proof master then decided if a third proof was needed. If the examination was satisfactory, or perhaps even after a third proof shot, this proof mark was applied. The third proof, if required, was fired with half the charge of the second shot. Pistol barrels were proofed with 1/3 the load prescribed for shotgun barrels.

It is conceivable that somewhere in southern Germany or Austria there exists one or more guns marked in this manner. While perhaps not valuable, they would be of interest because of the early Ferlach proof marks, which, to some extent are still in use today.

The proof law of June 23, 1891 made proof compulsory for all barrels manufactured in Austria-Hungary. Proof houses were established in Vienna, Prague, Weipert and Budapest. The existing proof house in Ferlach was continued, and a subsidiary proof house of the Vienna facilities was established at Steyr. This house used the same stamp as the Vienna proof house.

The new proof law also recognized three different proof steps or procedures for shotgun barrels. The unfinished barrels underwent first proof, the joined barrels of double-barrel shotguns, combination guns, and drillings underwent second proof, while finished shotguns and handguns had to undergo the third proof.

A side-by-side shotgun or a combination gun, after undergoing the complete series of proof shots, would show all three of the proof marks, a single-barrel shotgun would carry first and third proof marks, while a handgun would display only the third proof mark. Barrels which did not pass proof were destroyed. Barrels which passed proof were marked with the proof mark as well as the bore diameter in millimeters (mm), with fractions of a millimeter being marked by the decimal system (e. g.: 7.62 mm). After the third proof, the barrel was also marked with the corresponding proof number in the proof house record book.

Each of these proofs consisted of a stiffer load than used in the preceding shot. The propellant was a fine-grained Austrian black powder (Jagd- und Scheibenpulver Nr. 1). For the first two proofs a lead cylinder was used as projectile, while the third proof load called for the use of a prescribed amount of lead shot. The first proof load was designed to produce twice the normal chamber pressure as created by a standard load; the second proof increased the pressure by 2/3 over that of the standard load, and the third shot increased the pressure by another 1/3. During the first and the second proof firing, the open rear of the barrel was closed by means of a temorary bolt, but for the third proof firing, the gun had to be completed and ready for use.

As example, let us again fall back on a 16 gauge barrel.

Proof No. 1: 148.15 grains of black powder and a 888.88 grain lead cylinder.

Proof No. 2: 123.46 grains of black powder and a 740.74 grain lead cylinder.

Proof No. 3: 98.76 grains of black powder and a 592.59 grain load of lead shot where the standard load consisted of 69.4–71.2 grains of black powder behind a load of lead shot weighing 462.96 grains.

When a comparison is made between this proof load system and that used in Belgium or Great Britain, it immediately becomes apparent that the Austro-Hungarian proof was not a strong one. The Austrians, however, have maintained that their black powder is especially fine-grained, hence was stronger and delivered about twice the energy of the earlier, coarse powder they had been using. This coarser powder was more potent than any other powder used anywhere for proof loads. In contrast to other powders used in proof loads, even in stiff charges, according to the Austrian proof master, the coarser powder burned much more evenly than any other proof powder tested.

There was no special proof for rifled barrels, and these were proofed in the same manner as were the smoothbored ones.

As with the German law, enacted at about the same time, there was no smokeless powder proof. On August 23, 1899, decree Number 174 appeared in the official records. Initiated by the appropriate government department, it called for a weak semi-smokeless proof on a voluntary basis. The regulation prescribed an increase of 50 per cent in pressure over the standard black powder load. If this pressure level was really reached, it would represent a very strong proof, especially when compared with the relatively mild black powder pressure levels. Arms proofed with semi-smokeless powder were given a special mark which in effect is a combination of the letters N and P, plus the beginning letter of the proof house where the proof firing was performed.

The proof marks in use are those decreed by the passage of the law in 1891 and the decree of 1899. Here it becomes essential to differentiate the Austrian proof marks with some care.

Guns proofed after the first World War at proof houses located in Austria carry as third proof a two-headed eagle with the number of the proof house shown on the breast plate. Ferlach was Number 1, Prague was Number 2, Weipert was Number 3, and Vienna had Number 4. Budapest, however, went its own way and used a totally different proof mark.

AUSTRO-HUNGARIAN PROOF MARKS

These marks were in use after the law of 1891 and when the decree of 1899 went into effect, and remained in use until about 1928.

Ferlach Prague Weipert Vienna Budapest

The proof house* at Budapest used , while all the other Austrian proof houses used a different mark, the identical one being used for all four of them. All guns in trade which had not been proofed when the proof law went into effect in 1891, were given a special mark.**

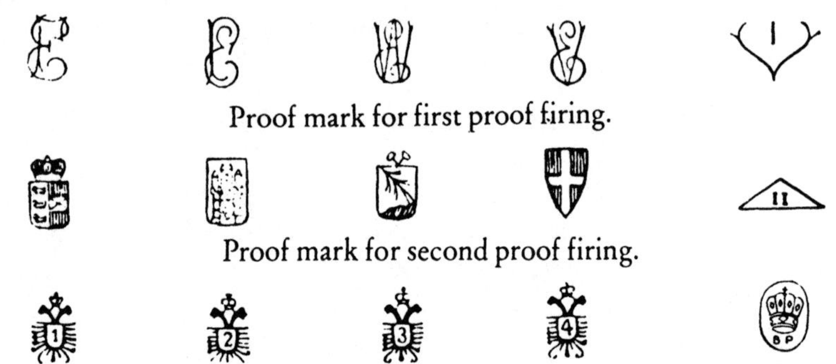

Proof mark for first proof firing.

Proof mark for second proof firing.

Proof mark for the third proof firing or the viewing which replaced the third proof firing.

* In Hungary the proof law of November 3, 1891, decree 34, was in effect and this is almost the same as the Austrian proof law. No change in Hungarian proof law was made until 1929.

** In contrast to the German proof law, any gun marked with the interim unproofed mark had to be submitted for proof within the year. Thus, in effect, such arms were only temporarily exempt from proof.

Ferlach	Prague	Weipert	Vienna	Budapest
NPF	NPP	NPW	NPV	NPB

MARKS USED FOR SEMI-SMOKELESS POWDER PROOF

Choke-bored barrels were marked “NICHT FÜR KUGEL” (Not For Ball) in Austria, but in Hungary these were stamped “NEM GOLYONAK.” Guns proofed with semi-smokeless powder also were marked with the weight of the projectile used in proof.

AFTER WORLD WAR I

The end of World War 1 also saw the end of the Austro-Hungarian Empire. Austria, Hungary and Czechoslovakia went their own ways, Yugoslavia also split off, and no proof for this country is known. At first, the three independent states retained the old proof marks, but these were changed at a later date. More about these marks a bit later on.

AUSTRIA

In post-WW I Austria, the proof law of 1891 was retained. However, the supervising agencies now were the commerce and finance departments in conjunction with the Chancellor, thus effectively side-stepping any attempt to have the cumbersome machinery of Parliament get into the act. The new regulation appeared on August 14, 1929, became effective on September 1, 1929.

Proof was now divided into two parts: the preliminary or provisional and the final proof. The preliminary proof was purely a material testing system designed to exclude defective barrels during manufacture, thus saving time, labor and costs. The final proofing was done while the gun was still in the white but otherwise fully functional. Once the gun passed proof, it was blued and perhaps engraved.

Preliminary Proof

Long guns: The unfinished barrel is proofed with the load listed in the proof tables. Barrels earmarked for single-barrel guns, once they have passed proof, are then marked appropriately. Barrels which will be used for doubles or multi-barrel guns are then soldered with whatever other barrel or barrels will eventually make up the gun. Still in the white, the barrels then undergo yet another preliminary proof. The proof load is again determined from the same proof tables. Once the barrels have passed this proof, they are stamped with the preliminary proof mark. Barrels for Flobert guns need not undergo preliminary proof and are proofed only once with the charge prescribed for final proof.

The bore diameter is recorded in millimeters and tenths of millimeters in the records of the proof house.

Handguns: Barrels destined for handguns do not undergo preliminary proof. They are proofed only once, during the final proof firing, and this occurs after the barrel is completely finished.

The incomplete barrels which have undergone preliminary proof are given this proof mark. The mark for Vienna  is also used for the branch proof house at Steyr. The proof house at Ferlach used this mark

. Thus, the mark on barrels for single-barrel guns indicate that the barrel has passed preliminary proof. On barrels for double or multi-barrel guns, the mark indicates that the barrel has passed the first of several proof firings.

In the proof mark for the second step in the preliminary proofing of barrels for double and multi-barrel guns, no differentiation is made between smoothbored and rifled barrels, but the proof charges are listed under different headings in the proof tables. Again, Vienna and Steyr share proof marks  , while the Ferlach proof house used this mark 

In the case of final proof for black powder guns, the following points should be noted.

Shotguns are tested with the international chamber pressure system, the load being used creating an average chamber pressure of 8818 psi. The Austrian powder and shot charges for proof are lighter than their Belgian counterparts, but they nevertheless develop the same amount of chamber pressure.

Guns with rifled barrels designed for black powder use are proofed with a proof load which develops pressures 30 per cent in excess over the standard load. Revolvers are also tested with a 30 per cent overload, one shot being fired in each chamber. Flobert rifles are proofed only once with the final proof and here proof consists of using the longest possible cartridge case that can be inserted into the chamber. The case is filled to the upper edge with powder and the usual bullet is seated on top of the charge.

Shotguns that will be used with semi-smokeless powder must first undergo the final black powder proof, then are further tested with a proof load using semi-smokeless powder. Chamber pressure of a gun, 16 gauge or larger, must be at least 12,800 psi while in the smaller gauges the pressure must reach no less than 14,223 psi.

Rifled barrels for semi-smokeless powder are proofed with a semi-smokeless proof powder which creates the usual 30 per cent excess pressure over the standard load.

Revolvers are proofed with a special semi-smokeless proof powder, and one round is fired in each chamber of the cylinder. The chamber pressure developed by the proof load has to exceed the chamber pressure of the standard cartridge by 30 per cent.

All arms which have passed final black powder proof are marked with this stamp, regardless of whether the barrel is smoothbored or rifled, long or short. The Vienna and the Steyr proof house used , while Ferlach used the same eagle but with the number "1" on the breast plate.

The proof marks of smokeless proof are stamped on the appropriate gun and are placed next to the other proof marks. The final proof mark of the Vienna proof house carries the number "2", similar to the final proof mark used by the proof house in Prague. The final proof mark used by the Ferlach proof house differs markedly from that used by the Vienna house. In addition to the compulsory proof, whoever submits a gun to the proof house can ask for a stronger or re-enforced proof with semi-smokeless powder. Such barrels carry this mark.

Guns imported from foreign countries, and that includes Germany, must undergo new proof tests unless the Government of Austria accepts the foreign proof mark. If such a foreign gun must undergo proof again at one of the Austrian proof houses, this mark (F) is applied to the gun.

Imported barrels which do not carry officially accepted proof marks must undergo Austrian proof before they can be incorporated into a gun made in this country. If the barrel is destined for a single-barrel shotgun, it must pass first proof; if it is to be used for a double-barrel or multi-barrel gun, the imported barrel must pass first and second preliminary proof. Finished and completed rifles imported from abroad with a barrel or barrels which have undergone only preliminary proof, must undergo final proof in Austria. After passing proof, they are marked with (F).

Should, however, preliminary proof marks be missing from the barrel or barrels, they must undergo the second preliminary proof before they can be admitted to the final proof stage.

After successfully passing the preliminary proof, the barrels are marked on the flats with the proof number. After passing final proof, the final proof number is stamped on the right underneath side of each barrel, and each barrel is also marked with the bore or gauge.

Finished guns which are already serially numbered at the factory are not marked with the proof number.

Smoothbored, choked barrels are marked on the lower right side with the word "CHOKE," and all barrels chambered for shells longer than 65 mm (2.56"), are marked with the gauge and the length of the shell for which the barrel is chambered, for instance 12/70, where 70 mm represents 2 3/4 -inch.

AUSTRIAN PROOF LAW OF 1940

After the annexation of Austria by Germany, the German proof law became effective on June 7, 1939, and the German proof law replaced all other proof regulations for the Sudetenland after its annexaction by Reich edict on June 1, 1940. For details about German proof and proof regulations, please refer to the section on German proof. Reference is made here to some sections of the law of June 7, 1939, as it applies to Austria.

Included were:

a) the proof order of March 7, 1940;
b) publication of minimum groove width for chamber pressure determination for rifle cartridges of March 20, 1940;
c) publication of chamber and cartridge dimensions for hand-held arms on April 10, 1940;
d) the order of January 22, 1940, to form a proof board.

The government proof houses and their marks were as follows:
Ferlach, as before, the official coat of arms of Carinthia, see above.
Vienna, the coat of arms of the city of Vienna as before, see above.

Weipert, the same as before. For the proof marks of Weipert prior to 1940 and after 1945, see under Czechoslovakia.

AUSTRIAN PROOF MARKS 1945–1951

In 1945 the Austrian government decided to use new and more modern proof marks. The German proof law of 1939, introduced in Austria in 1940, was repealed and the old proof law of 1929 was reintroduced in a somewhat simpler form and with changed proof marks.

The mark for the first preliminary proof, for the semi-smokeless proof and also the re-enforced proof with semi-smokeless powder remained as they had been. The second preliminary proof was eliminated. For multi-barreled guns, the second preliminary was replaced by the first preliminary proof, and what formerly was the third or final black powder proof, became now the second and also final proof. The proof mark—the double-headed eagle with the number in the breast plate—remained. The modern eagle lacks the crown and now holds a hammer in the left and a sickle in the right talon.

The proof marks used during this time span were as follows: For guns which had passed the first or the preliminary proof, the Vienna proof house used this stamp, while the Ferlach facilities used . These are the same proof marks as specified in the proof law of 1929.

These marks were used on guns which had passed the second or final black powder proof— represents the Vienna installation, while was the Ferlach mark. The marks were stamped onto the rear of the barrel and on all important parts of the gun.

The proof marks for semi-smokeless powder are the same as specified for the law of 1929, with NPV indicating the Vienna proof house, and NPF that at Ferlach.

The proof marks PV indicating re-enforced proof with semi-smokeless powder are the same marks as specified in the 1929 law.

THE PROOF LAW SINCE 1951

The new Austrian proof law of June 13, 1951, became effective on July 1 of that year, and the procedural methods were published on October 27 of that year. Although relatively brief, it is quite easy to see that the basic concept of this law is based on the German proof law of 1939. The new Austrian proof law also follows the agreement made in Brussels in 1914.

One of the more interesting aspects of the law is that all arms in the country fall under the proof rules providing they do not carry foreign proof marks which are recognized and accepted by the Austrian government. This rule is primarily directed against the great number of foreign guns which came into Austria during the post-war occupation, and specifically against those guns which come from countries which do not have proof laws, such as Russia, Poland, Romania, Yugoslavia, etc. Among those post-war imports are also a great many illegal guns.

Another feature of the new Austrian proof law is that a gun that has undergone complete proof, will after a number of years, have to undergo re-proof. At the moment that time span has not been determined. This is a very reasonable and well thought out part of the law since it will tend to eliminate, at least gradually, some of the older black powder guns which constitute a public danger to shooters. Unfortunately, the applicable sections of the German proof law have not been incorporated in this section of the Austrian law. It seems very unlikely that in the relatively short time the German law has been in effect that all of these old guns have been removed from the scene, hence this must be considered a drawback of the 1951 law, and apparently the law makers who wrote the law and the proof regulations were aware of this shortcoming.

Mentioned only are "shotgun barrels" for shells loaded with smokeless powder, which are to be tested with one load of black powder and two shots of smokeless powder during final proofing. For shotgun barrels a preliminary proof is prescribed, this to be done with one load of black powder where chamber pressure at a specified location—location 1—must reach, by means of the international gas pressure determination system, no less than 11,378 psi. At the same location, the chamber pressure of the final proof of shotgun barrels to be proofed with black powder must reach 9956 psi. For barrels which must be proofed with semi-smokeless powder—and here the law calls it "smokeless"—the chamber pressure must reach 12,800 psi for 16 gauge or larger barrels, while for smaller gauge barrels, the prescribed pressure is 14,223 psi.

Very good is the rule that any faults that could affect the safety of the barrel, which could result in an eventual return of the barrel without proof mark; this includes soldering joints with a metal melting at very high temperatures, sweating or brazing joints of parts exposed to wear and tear, and the unintentional loosening of locks. Alterations, repairs, or restorations may affect a gun to such an extent that the gun may have to be re-submitted for proof; such jobs as installing a telescopic sight, changing the magazine, any alterations on the bore of the gun, and heat treating metal parts fall under the new proof regulations. This is designed to eliminate any possibility of sloppy gunsmithing which could endanger gun or shooter.

The proof of centerfire rifle barrels and barrels of self-loading pistols is accomplished with two shots of smokeless powder loads. All other guns for which smokeless cartridges are on the market are proofed with one smokeless powder load; all others are proofed with one load of black powder.

The proof marks under the new law are the same as existed under the 1945 rules, and their usage is also identical, hence they are not being repeated here.

Very much like the Belgian, German and Spanish law, the Austrian law makes provisions for proofing shotshells. These are tested for functioning, maximum chamber pressure developed, maintenance of dimensional specifications and packing.

The proof houses are further empowered within the framework of the technical capabilities in the firearms field to undertake testing of shooting products of other kinds as well, and to undertake also metallurgic and physical studies if they concern shooting and firearms.

PROOF LAW OF 1958

On May 9, 1958, and on February 12 of 1962, the scope of the Austrian proof law was expanded. According to it, all firearms and power-actuated tools must undergo final proof. This includes: flare guns, cattle killing devices, stud drivers, bolt and cable cutters and barrel inserts. Excluded are those devices designed exclusively for blank cartridges and antique guns.

Since 1962, the proof law permits replacement of the preliminary proof by a non-destructive material test, such as Magnaflux or X-ray.

For shotguns with chambers longer than 70 mm ($2\frac{3}{4}$ "), the permissible chamber pressure must exceed the normal prescribed proof pressure by at least 1422 psi. The re-enforced semi-smokeless proof of shotguns must be performed with enough powder to produce at least 17,068 psi.

In proofing centerfire rifles with cartridges developing a maximum gas pressure of 46,936 psi or even more, the usual 30 per cent excessive pressure requirement is waived. Such guns are proofed with loads which develop at least 14,223 psi more chamber pressure than the strongest commercial cartridge in use.

Whoever submits guns to the proof house must also submit the load data for the commercial ammunition, all dimensional data, maximum pressure, etc., if the proof master is not familiar with the ammunition for which the gun or guns are chambered. Moreover, the person requesting proof must also furnish cartridges, cartridge case and loading components, including loading dies if commercial ammunition is not available.

Every gun submitted for proof must be marked with the maker's name, caliber or gauge, and the quality of the steel used.

CZECHOSLOVAKIA

Until 1931, the Czech proof houses not only used the old proof facilities at Prague and Weipert, but they continued to use the old Austro-Hungarian proof marks. There are some German sources who maintain that, as early as 1928 the proof mark of the third proof—the double-headed eagle with the number "2" for Prague and "3" for Weipert on the breast plate—had been replaced by the Bohemian double-tailed lion with the numbers "1" and "2". However, the author has not succeeded in obtaining official confirmation of this claim. The proof marks of both houses are reproduced here as they appear in Col. Goddard's small brochure on European proof marks. This lion  is the mark of the Prague proof house, while this indicates the Weipert facilities.

The proof law now in use in Czechoslovakia dates back to December 17, 1931, which became effective on January 1, 1932. The rules of proof date to December 22, 1931.

Perhaps the most important aspect of the Czech proof law is that all firearms in which semi-smokeless powder can be used, must also be proofed with that propellant. Black powder proof is used only as preliminary proof of the unfinished barrels and as final proof only for such guns which, because of their weak construction or for other reasons, such as historical value, cannot be proofed with semi-smokeless powder charges. Rifled barrels and guns for use with semi-smokeless powder and jacketed bullets must be proofed with semi-smokeless powder and jacketed bullets.

The proofing of shotgun barrels consists first of the voluntary proof of the unfinished barrel or barrels with black powder at a minimum chamber pressure of 15,645 psi. The second and obligatory proof with black powder with barrels either still in the white, or in the case of multi-barreled guns, the barrels already joined, the minimum chamber pressure must be 11,378 psi. The third compulsory black powder proof is performed when the gun is finished but not yet blued, and international standards call for a chamber pressure of 8818 psi. Finally, all guns that have passed the third proof, undergo a fourth proof firing, this one compulsory, with semi-smokeless powder and a minimum chamber pressure of 14,223 psi, the case length not exceeding 2.559" (65 mm). With longer cases, the pressure limits are increased.

Autoloading shotguns are proofed with two shots. The first shot consists of the load used for the voluntary preliminary proof firing, while the second shot uses a standard, commercially loaded shell. The reasoning behind the third proof with black powder is not quite clear and may well be a forgotten part of the old Austro-Hungarian proof rules.

Arms with rifled barrels are proofed only with semi-smokeless powder, and only those guns designed for black powder are proofed with that propellant. Proof is accomplished with three shots, where the first two must have 30 per cent more chamber pressure than the standard cartridge, and the third proof consists of firing such a cartridge, the brand of the round used being left to the discretion of the proof master.

Only if the gun is proofed with black powder is the second proof with the standard use load omitted. All other requirements, however, remain the same. Flobert guns, up to 9 mm caliber, are proofed with only one shot. Here the proof load consists of filling the cartridge case full of black powder, but the load may not exceed 15.432 grains (1.0 Gm.) of powder and the shot charge may not exceed 123.46 grains (8.0 Gm.). Semiautomatic pistols are proofed with two rounds loaded with semi-smokeless powder. Both shots must produce an excess pressure of 50 per cent of the standard or commercial cartridge, and guns must be submitted for proof completely ready for use. Revolvers designed for black powder cartridges are proofed with a caseful of black powder and the standard bullets for the gun, with all chambers being loaded and fired. The pressure level of the proof load must exceed the normal pressure of this cartridge by 30 per cent.

Revolvers designed for semi-smokeless propellants are proofed to a 50 per cent excess chamber pressure over the normal pressure created by the standard load.

Since 1931 the Czech proof houses have been using the following proof marks:

 Voluntary proof of unfinished barrels, also known as first proof.

Second obligatory proof, barrel in the white, proof with black powder. Barrels for multi-barreled guns must already be joined.

Third, obligatory proof with black powder under international regulations. This mark is also used to indicate proof of rifled barrels on handguns and rifles which are designed for black powder only; also indicates final proof for shotguns.

Mark used for the obligatory semi-smokeless proof of shotguns, also known as fourth proof.

Mark used for the obligatory, semi-smokeless proof of rifled barrels for handguns and long guns.

Aside from the shown proof marks, any gun that underwent complete proof is also marked with the caliber or gauge designation as well as the proof number recorded for the gun in the records of the proof house.

The proof marks shown were used by the Prague proof house as well as by the Weipert facilities, with the latter using the marks from 1931–1938. To differentiate its work from the Prague office, a star was used by the Weipert proof master directly above the proof house mark.

During the years 1938–1945, Weipert used the German proof marks of the 1891 and the 1939 proof laws respectively. In 1945 the Weipert facilities were closed, and new facilities were supposed to be opened in Brno. However, no details about this proof house or its mark have become available.

After 1945 the old Czech proof marks were put back into use and are still in use today as far as we know. The following table gives the reader the complete picture of Czech proof at a glance.

TYPE OF FIREARM		TYPE OF PROOF	PROOF POWDER	TIME													
				1891–1899		1899–1919		1919–1931		1931–1939		1940–1945		1945–1955	1946–1952	1955–1962	1962–1972
				PRAGUE	WEIPERT	PRAGUE	WEIPERT	PRAGUE	WEIPERT	PRAGUE	WEIPERT	PRAGUE	WEIPERT	PRAGUE	BRNO	PRAGUE	PRAGUE
SINGLE BARRELS		OBLIGATORY	BLACK POWDER								SAME MARK AS PRAGUE, BUT WITH STAR		MARKS FOLLOW RULES OF THIRD REICH		SAME MARK AS PRAGUE, BUT WITH STAR OR		
		OPTIONAL	BLACK POWDER									P1					
DOUBLE BARRELS		OBLIGATORY	BLACK POWDER									P2					
		OPTIONAL	BLACK POWDER, AFTER 1962 VOLUNTARY														
SHOTGUNS	BLACK POWDER	OBLIGATORY	BLACK POWDER														
		OPTIONAL	BLACK POWDER														
	SMOKELESS POWDER	OBLIGATORY	SMOKELESS POWDER							N		N		N		N	
		OPTIONAL	SMOKELESS POWDER			NP	NW	NP	NW								
	SINGLE PROOF	OBLIGATORY	OPTIONAL														N
HUNTING RIFLES	BLACK POWDER	OBLIGATORY	BLACK POWDER														
	SMOKELESS POWDER	OBLIGATORY	SMOKELESS POWDER														
	SMOKELESS POWDER	OPTIONAL	SMOKELESS POWDER			NP	NW	NP	NW								
REVOLVERS		OBLIGATORY	BLACK POWDER														
		OPTIONAL	SMOKELESS POWDER			NP	NW	NP	NW								
		OBLIGATORY	SMOKELESS POWDER														

TYPE OF FIREARM	TYPE OF PROOF	PROOF POWDER	TIME													
			1891–1899		1899–1919		1919–1931		1931–1939		1940–1945		1945–1955	1946–1952	1955–1962	1962–1972
			PRAGUE	WEIPERT	PRAGUE	WEIPERT	PRAGUE	WEIPERT	PRAGUE	WEIPERT	PRAGUE	WEIPERT	PRAGUE	BRNO	PRAGUE	PRAGUE
SEMIAUTOMATIC PISTOLS	OBLIGATORY	BLACK POWDER														
	OPTIONAL	SMOKELESS POWDER			NP	NW	NP	NW								
	OBLIGATORY	SMOKELESS POWDER														
SMALLBORE RIFLES	OBLIGATORY	BLACK POWDER														
	OBLIGATORY	SMOKELESS POWDER													N UP TO 1960; SINCE 1960	
FLOBERT RIFLES	OBLIGATORY	BLACK POWDER													N	N
SALON GUNS	OBLIGATORY	BLACK POWDER														N
STUD DRIVERS	OBLIGATORY	USUALLY SMOKELESS														
GASGUNS&AMMUNITION	OBLIGATORY														ČSR	CSSR
OTHER AMMUNITION	OBLIGATORY														WITHOUT STAMP	CSSR

IMPORTATION MARKS

PRAGUE — PRAGUE – ARMS IMPORTED FROM BELGIUM

WEIPERT — WEIPERT – ARMS IMPORTED FROM BELGIUM

PRAGUE — PRAGUE – GERMAN ARMS IMPORTED INTO THE PROTECTORATE

HUNGARY

Up to 1928 Hungary used the Austro-Hungarian proof marks. In that year new proof marks were introduced and according to European sources, the same marks are still in use today. Further details and conditions of proof are not readily available, but it can be assumed that they are in accordance with other European proofs and proof methods.
The Hungarian proof marks are as follows:

Proof of unfinished barrels.*

Proof for barrels in the white, destined for multi-barrel guns,*

Obligatory final black powder proof.

Proof for all guns with semi-smokeless powder.

Nem Golyonak "Not for Ball" is marked on all barrels with choke. In such barrels only projectiles suitable for the choking may be used.

1057/28 The number under which the proof of gun is entered in proof book, here 1057; second number indicates year, in this case 1928.

1026,8 The barrel weight in grams and tenths of grams, in this case 1026 8/10th Gm. or 36.22 ounces.

17,5 Bore diameter in millimeters and tenths of millimeters. Here bore diameter is 17.5 mm or 0.6889 inch. According to international rules, this measurement is taken between 15–22 cm or 5.9–8.66 inches from the standing breech.

* These proofs are voluntary.

In considering proof in Hungary, it must be kept in mind that after the treaty of 1867, Hungary became an independent state within Austria-Hungary. The Austrian emperor was also the Hungarian king, and Hungarian independence became apparent in the form of minor formalities. For instance, the Hungarian proof law of the time is simply a translated copy of the Austrian proof law, but the proof marks differ markedly.

1. The Hungarian proof law was enacted on November 2, 1891.
2. The law went into effect on May 18, 1892 and remained basically unchanged until 1971.
3. The rules of proof, initiated by the minister of trade, order number 27290 of 1892, was changed in 1928. The new version, under order number 89718, of 1928, became effective on July 10, 1928. The proof basically follows the outlines established by the International Proof Conference in Belgium in 1914.
4. The sketch of the Hungarian crown in the proof law differs considerably from the actual mark.
   a. The sketch of the temporary proof in the law appeared thusly, but in actuality looked like this and lacks the letter "K".

   b. The sketch of the proof mark for final proof looks like this but as seen on guns, it appears like this.

B.p.

5. The correct mark for semi-smokeless proof was: FN — these are the first letters of the words "füst nélküli" which means "smokeless."

The following changes took place in the proof rules and these were in force, as far as it is known, until April 1, 1971. Instead of the crown (4b) the following signs were in use: from 1949 until 1956, and from 1957 until 1971:

On April 1, 1971 a new proof rule went into effect (No. 9/1970 BM-KGM.) Now used are:

1. Temporary and voluntary proof of barrels in the white: 
2. Final proof of gun, either in the white or blued, with semi-smokeless powder (N = Nitro): 
3. Re-proof:

SUMMARY

All firearms proofed for semi-smokeless powder in Austria, Czechoslovakia or Hungary must be marked with the letter "N" and the initial of the proof house where the gun was tested. Firearms proofed under the proof laws of 1928–1931 and later guns, if in good condition, can be used with semi-smokeless ammunition of the suitable size of German manufacture without problem. Suitability of guns can easily be determined on hand of the proof marks shown on each firearm.

A great many of the older arms are in sound condition and can be used, but it is recommended that such a gun be examined by a competent gunsmith before firing. Should there be a question about the condition of the gun, it is best to have the gun re-proofed in Germany.

GERMANY

As must be expected from a country where the art of gun making has long been recognized, references to proof in Germany date back to the Romans. Many of the early marks seen are City or Guild marks and not proof marks as we know them. These early City marks, such as those of Nürnberg, Augsburg, Amsterdam and Utrecht (both once German cities), merely indicated that the gun bearing such a mark was made in that town and had, in some cases, passed the gimlet-eyed inspection of a master gunsmith. The mark, however, did not signify the soundness of the barrel which, after all, is the crux of any firearm.

The first of the true proof marks have been traced to 1850, and it seems reasonable to assume that those three discovered marks do not represent all of the German proof marks of that period. The first known Suhl proof mark dates to 1600 and consists of the City mark with a somewhat stylized chicken *(Henne* in German). The Henne is a part of the escutcheon of Count Henneberg whose estates were in Suhl. SVL and later SUL were used by the town as City stamp, and from 1655, the city employed a special man whose sole job it was to fire one or two shots from every barrel produced in the city. Therefore, the above marks should be considered as true proof marks rather than as identification marks of the gun maker.

Military arms made in Suhl between 1600 and 1690—and this despite the fact that the town and all gun making establishments were destroyed by a troop of Imperial Croats in 1634—bear the escutcheon of the town, a footprint with an imbedded ax. The same mark was used after the proof law of 1939 became effective, and is still in use today. There was a hiatus in the activities of the Suhl proof house during the 18th century, and it was not until 1893 that the royal Prussian government re-established the Suhl proof facilities.

Noteworthy are the proof marks of the city of Essen. In 1545 a town decree was issued that ordered every barrel maker to afix his mark to each barrel he made. Stock makers and lock makers had to swear that they would not use any barrel that lacked the maker's stamp, and in 1544 a city ordinance was passed which required that every firearm sold in the city bear the city's proof mark. As in Suhl, the town engaged the services of a man who was responsible for the proofing of the guns. Unfortunately, almost nothing is known about those proof regulations and conditions under which the guns were tested. The Essen mark was a sword with a rounded pommel. Stockel, in his classic work on proof and maker marks, records two marks for the town of Essen for that period. This makes the Essen proof rules the first in Europe, even earlier than those of London or Liege.

In the year 1676 it was decreed that barrels made outside the town could not be marked with the town's stamp, thus, in effect offering probably also the first consumer protection regulation. All barrels have to be marked with the caliber, this to be expressed in number of lead balls per pound of lead. All craftsmen working on a gun, and that included the stock maker, lock maker and even the furniture maker, had to impress his mark on his work and/or parts. In 1695 the proof rules specified that the proof mark must be applied to the upper part of the barrel so that it would be readily visible, and barrels which passed proof especially well were marked with a crown above the sword. Up to the 18th century, many of the guns made in Essen bore not only the Essen proof mark, but also the marks of many gun makers. At the beginning of the 19th century, when Essen was under French rule, the mark "Manufacture d'Essen" appears, the factory using this mark having been founded in 1803. Arms made in this town enjoyed an excellent reputation and export, even to the United States, was lively until Napoleon and later the British import rules ruined this lucrative business.

After Napoleon's fall, the firearms industry of Essen declined, and in 1840 the last Essen rifle makers moved first to Saar in the Ruhr, and later to Erfurt where they became the nucleus of the future Erfurter Gewehrfabrik (Rifle Works). In the roster of master gunsmiths in Essen between the 16th and the 18th century, the name Krupp appears quite frequently.

The third German city to call for proof, this one for shotgun barrels, is Bourg (or possibly Berg) in the Duchy of Berg. Very little is known about either the proof rules or the mark used by this town, but town records of 1769 describe the excellence of the locally-made smoothbore barrels and cautions the users of such barrels to ascertain that any barrel they use have the mark of one of the local gunsmiths. Over 200 years ago, the town fathers warned that many cheap and poorly made barrels from Liege and Essen were being brought to Bourg and sold as having been made locally!

In the evolution of proof in Germany, the Imperial Prussian proof house at Solingen is the next one to be considered. Active since 1867, the mark consists of a stylized Prussian eagle with the letters "SP"—Solingen Probe or Solingen Proof—underneath, the entire mark being enclosed in an oval.

On November 30, 1890, the German Government submitted to the Reichstag (Parliament) the draft for a comprehensive proof law. The basic concept of this draft had its origins in the then current British and Belgian proof laws. According to official sources, the introduction of a proof law had been requested by the German sporting arms industry so that guns made in Germany could compete on the market place with guns imported from countries where proof laws existed—at that time, England, Belgium and Austria. Although this sounds logical and quite reasonable, it must be noted that the Belgian proof law of 1672 and the British one of 1813 and 1815 were allegedly introduced for the same reason. The arms industry in both countries opposed proof laws since it gave the government too much control over private enterprise. No literature or other material for the late '80s and early '90s about the pros and cons of proof appears to be available. Even Oberländer, in his works about the period, makes no mention about the acceptance of proof laws by industry, or by shooters and hunters.

Any information about this subject would, at best, be academic at this time, and the fact remains that a strict proof law was as essential then as it is today. The shortcomings of the first proof laws are now apparent, but it must not be forgotten that the first proof rules formed the basis for the German proof act of 1939 which is the best proof law ever written and thus has served as basis for proof acts in other countries.

On May 19, 1891, the German Reichstag passed the proof law, and the actual rules were made public on June 22, 1892, the proof rules becoming law on April 1, 1893. In its final form, the law deviated somewhat from the original concept—that is the British and Belgian proof—and now contained features which had not been considered earlier. The British proof law of 1887 and, as already mentioned, the Imperial Belgian order of 1891, made provisions for proof with semi-smokeless powder. The German law did make provisions for a voluntary proof where the person submitting a gun for proof could specify the type of powder to be used for proofing. However, the prescribed method for submitting gun and powder specifications were so complex as to make the voluntary proof virtually impossible. Georg Koch, in his comments about the law, in 1892 stated: "For instance, if proof of a 16 gauge barrel with Walsroder semi-smokeless powder is requested, the required proof load consists of 24.7 grains of powder and 926 grains of shot, while second proofing would require 49.4 grains of powder and 617.2 grains of shot." The load of 74.1 grains of powder with 926 grains of shot is more than adequate as proof in my opinion. In effect, it should be considered excessive since a great many barrels as well as locks have failed during proof, particularly since a load increase of 1.5 grains with nitro powders produces destructive effects.

The increasing use of nitro powders soon led to special barrel and lock proof rules, especially since the standards established for black powder were not applicable for nitro powders. It was not until 1912 that rules for semi-smokeless powder were changed so that the development of proof rules could progress and keep up with new technological advances. The greater weight of German shotguns when compared to the weight of foreign smoothbores, which then and later was a bone of contention, was in part responsible for some of the absurd proof rules.

The rules called for the proof load to be stamped on the upper surface of the barrel. For instance, the standard load of 34.0 grains of Schultze powder and 540.1 grains of shot was marked $\frac{\text{6,6 gr. Sch. P.}}{\text{70 gr. Bl.}}$ and this in turn led to a great many mistakes and burst barrels.

This is the weakest part of the proof law and requires close study. According to Article One, hand and shoulder guns of all types may only be offered for sale or introduced into commerce when the barrel and lock or action shows the prescribed proof marks, thus indicating that the gun has undergone proof at one of the official proof house. Not included are firearms for scientific use or guns which are of historic or artistic interest and certainly will not be fired. Such firearms may be traded and sold freely and without restrictions. Although this sounds reasonable, it most certainly has caused problems since many a collector has fired one or more guns from his collection, thus violating the law without being aware of the existence of the article within the law. And how many times have gun collectors fired each other's gun to see how the gun function, how severe recoil might be or simply just for the enjoyment and fun of firing such a gun? How many young hunters started with grandpappy's muzzleloader although centerfire repeaters were in common use? Such an heirloom may well have been used to learn the basic art of shooting and hunting, and more than one youngster used such a black powder gun for several years during the hunting seasons. In the strictest sense of the law, if such a gun is being used, the use is punishable by law.

The very same Article has been incorporated in the proof law of 1939, and the same rule is still on the books today!

I am not aware of any violators being prosecuted under the law, and today, possession as well as use of such guns under conditions which cannot be interpreted as being public or commercial—this would include shooting such a gun but without witnesses—is legal.

According to Koch, it is questionable if such a firearm may be sold by a private citizen. A gun shop may not do so, but an antique store may do so legally.

During the discussions in Parliament, there were attempts made to exclude from proof the cheap export guns which are of very poor quality. Fortunately, these attempts failed and compulsory proof for all firearms became law. Exempt from German proof are all those firearms which were proofed and so marked by a foreign proof house, providing the foreign proof was at least equally as strong as the German proof. As will be seen under Belgian proof, this rule excluded the Liege proof system, and consequently, Belgium had to strengthen the proof regulations so that Belgian guns would be acceptable in Germany without having to undergo re-proof in Germany before being sold here. Thanks to the re-written proof regulations, the Belgian proof mark has been recognized in Germany since 1893.

It is important to note that military small arms, and that includes foreign guns accepted by means of proof firing by a military board or commission, need not be re-proofed when sold in Germany, either by a store or by a private individual. However, re-proof becomes mandatory if the gun has undergone either a change in caliber or some sort of action alteration—this would include rechambering, even for an "improved" caliber. Military weapons, withdrawn from such supply sources as armories and sold to the public at large, must be proofed and marked suitable before such a sale is legal.

Article Two states that the proof test consists of firing the gun with a re-enforced standard load. Muzzleloading pistols and revolvers must undergo only one proof firing. For all other firearms, two proof firings are required, the first one while the barrel is still in the rough, the second when the barrel or barrels have been finished, joined in the case of a multi-barrel gun, and the lock has been installed. It is possible for a person submitting a gun in such condition for proofing, to have the request for a single proof honored. In such instances, the condition of the barrels is tested as in second proof, but the proof load is the load prescribed for first proof. Such barrels are marked B. The responsibility for possible damages to barrel or barrels, produced by the re-enforced load, rests with the person submitting the gun for proof.

Proof mark for smoothbored shotgun barrels. 

Proof mark for rifled barrels. 

As in the British proof law, choke-bored barrels undergo a different proof than cylinder or open-bored barrels. Choke-bored shotgun muzzles are measured for bore size 8.6-inch (22 cm) ahead of the standing breech, all other barrels having this measurement taken at the muzzle. Choke-bored barrels must be proofed twice. If the choked section of the choke-bored barrel was smooth, that is unrifled, the barrel is proofed with the load prescribed for the bore corresponding to the bore of the rear of the barrel. If, however, the choked section of the barrel is wholly or even partially rifled, the barrel is to be proofed with a lead projectile, conical in the forward 1/3 of its length, and weighing 1 1/2 times the weight of the corresponding shot charge. Proof and service load data are obtained from the tables contained in the proof law.

Below are listed the loads for the most common smoothbored barrels:

		1st PROOF/gr		2nd PROOF/gr		STANDARD LOAD/gr	
GAUGE	BORE DIAMETER/IN.	POWDER	SHOT	POWDER	SHOT	POWDER	SHOT
12	.73	268.5	1095.6	179.0	729.9	89.5	547.8
16	.66	226.8	873.5	151.2	581.8	75.6	436.7
20	.61	203.7	765.4	135.8	510.8	67.9	382.7
24	.58	166.7	655.9	111.1	436.7	55.6	327.9
28	.55	166.7	655.9	111.1	436.7	55.6	327.9
32	.53	125.0	438.3	83.3	291.7	41.7	219.1

As in the British gauge/load tables—the German ones are patterned after them—the 4–10 gauges are divided into three sizes, the 11–17 gauges into two sizes, and the smaller gauges have but one gauge designation. In the tables appear completely useless gauge designations, such as 5 gauge and 7 gauge. Even more peculiar is the summary of the second load data table in which calibers for single projectile barrels are listed.

The number one table contains projectiles ranging in diameter from 1.5—1.669 inches to caliber .50, or .451—.454 inches, where each caliber has two or even three subdivisions and loads for the rifled barrel do not correspond with those for smoothbored barrels. The loads for caliber .454–.299 inches (7.62 mm), however, are not designated in the usual millimeter system used for rifled bores, but with the designation customarily employed for marking smoothbored barrels, that is caliber 51.05–172.28. The designation here is borrowed from the old British method of indicating the number of lead balls fitting the bore which can be cast from one pound of lead. Here, the higher the caliber designation, the smaller the ball cast; hence, the larger the number, the smaller the actual bore is. Just what possible value such a tabulation might have escapes even most experts and proof masters.

At the end of the load tables there is yet another listing of five re-enforced proof loads for rifled barrels, in this case Express barrels based on the same system. We list but a few of these tables here for comparison, and the differences between smoothbored and rifled barrels in the same caliber or bore diameter should be noted.

		1st PROOF/gr		2nd PROOF/gr		STANDARD LOAD/gr	
GAUGE OR CALIBER	BORE DIAMETER/in.	POWDER	BULLET	POWDER	BULLET	POWDER	BULLET
12	.728	282.4	1214.5	188.3	1214.5	94.1	910.5
20	.614	254.6	777.8	169.8	777.8	84.9	583.3
24	.577	254.6	714.5	169.8	714.5	84.9	535.5
24	.577	495.4	800.2	330.2	800.2	165.1	600.3*
37	.500	254.6	714.5	169.8	714.5	84.9	535.5
37	.500	449.1	586.4	299.4	586.4	149.7	439.8**
51.05	.449	254.6	714.5	169.8	714.5	84.9	535.5
51.05	.449	361.1	574.1	240.7	574.1	120.4	430.6***

* British .577 Express
** British .500 Express
*** British .450 Express

For calibers not listed in the proof load table, the person submitting a gun for proof must furnish load data in writing, as well as suitable cartridges, free of charge, to the proof master.

Proof mark of rifled barrels. [crown over G]

Article Three of the proof regulations covers not only all possible damages that can occur during proofing, but also how and when such firearms are to be completely destroyed, and in what instances such damages can be repaired and the gun re-submitted for proof.

This includes bulging of barrels or swelling or stretching of actions, and in such failures, the law prescribes that the damaged part be made useless either by sawing it apart or crushing it.

Article Four covers alterations of an already proofed firearm. These changes can occur in either the barrel, such as rechambering for an improved cartridge, or a change in the action or magazine so that the gun will handle a cartridge of a caliber different from that for which the gun was proofed. In such cases, the gun must undergo proof again, even if the barrel has not undergone any changes and has retained its original caliber. The mark for such a re-proof is crown over R.

Article Five covers such guns which were on dealer's shelves and warehouses when the proof law went into effect. As far as they could be located, the firearms were taken to the nearest proof house where they were given the crown over V mark crown over V, the V standing for *Vorrat* or supply. These guns were not actually proofed but merely given the mark. The Austrian proof rules were less lenient, and the Austrian *Vorrat*'s mark exempted the gun from proof for only one year. The owner of the gun had to submit the firearm to the proof house prior to the expiration of the year's grace period. In Germany most of these firearms were later submitted by the owners for a voluntary proof, since resale of even an almost new gun without proof was not acceptable to most gun buyers who soon learned to rely on the protection offered them by the proof laws.

Article six specifies that firearms with the crown over V mark, if no barrel or action alterations have been made, need not be proofed again. The same rule applies to firearms imported into Germany and bearing proof marks of proof houses with standards acceptable to the German proof law. Similarly, military weapons either made by an arms plant with acceptable standards or weapons made for military use by a commercial plant, need not undergo proof again providing they passed proof before, the proof being acceptable to the German proof masters.

Article Seven places the responsibility for proof procedures and proof marks on the Federal Council *(Bundesrat)*. The article further describes currently acceptable foreign proof marks and the countries issuing those marks. Proof for revolvers consists of firing one round each from each chamber in the cylinder. The proof load specified consists of a standard round with a beefed-up powder charge, the charge being increased as much as the powder space in the case allowed, without increasing the cartridge length and thus stopping cylinder rotation.

Muzzleloading pistols were proofed with a powder load exceeding 1½ times the standard load, and the standard projectile was used.

Guns for which a second proof was anticipated, were marked with  after passing first proof, the powder charge being threefold the normal charge. For second proof, the normal powder charge was doubled, and this mark  was applied, the eagle indicating second proof, and the crown over U being the *Untersuchungsstempel,* this indicating that the barrel had been examined or inspected. The prescribed proof load or shell cannot contain less powder or shot than the standard shell and the shot charge must consist of soft lead shot, measuring .087 inch or 2,2 mm in diameter. In other words, No. 7 shot is used. For the first proof, the shot charge weight is doubled from the standard load for this gauge, while for second proof, the shot charge is 1⅓ that of the standard load. In barrels designed to fire a single projectile—that is, rifled barrels—a soft lead cylinder is used as projectile. The weight of the cylinder is 1⅓ of the standard bullet for this caliber. For some not quite understood reason, the law specifies that the diameter of the lead cylinder be .008 inch (0,2 mm) less than bore diameter, and the forward portion of the cylinder must display a conical shape.

Article Eight is concerned with the rules pertaining to establishing proof houses and their functions. Article Nine covers the penalties for violation of the proof law, and Article Ten describes rules concerning the enactment of the proof law.

The shortcomings of this law are quite apparent. Rules concerning semi-smokeless powder are missing, although other countries had specific rules for this propellant, and neither shotgun nor rifle proof rules, especially rifle barrels to be used with jacketed bullets which had found acceptance then, are even mentioned. Obviously, the aim was to obtain a working rule for proof, and this also explains some of the proof loads which were below the performance levels of the standard rounds. In order to make proofing somewhat easier and more convenient, reduced loads and even slower burning powders were used. Even foreign powders were used since the German product was much hotter, and therefore made proofing sometimes difficult and even unpleasant.

Finally, the proof house at Zella-Mehlis introduced new proof rules on September 1, 1911, and the proof house at Suhl, in April 1912, adopted the Zella-Mehlis rules.

According to the new regulations, smoothbored and rifled barrels were tested with special proof powders which were produced by the *Köln-Rottweiler Pulverfabrik* (Cologne-Rottweiler Powder Works). These powders, from a 16 gauge barrel, with 28.5 grains of powder behind 463.0 grains of shot, produced a chamber pressure of 12,800 psi, and from a 12 gauge barrel with 36.3 grains of powder and 540.1 grains of shot, the pressure also was 12,800 psi.

For rifled barrels, a powder was used that in the Infantry Model 88, with 42.4 grains of powder behind a 226.8 grain jacketed bullet, recorded a chamber pressure of 56,892 psi. Thus, the rules of proof were simplified, the proof marks remained the same, and a new mark "NITRO" or

N
Nitro

was added for semi-smokeless proofed barrels. Shotguns designed for semi-smokeless powder were tested during second proof with a powder load, behind the standard shot charge, which produced a chamber pressure of 12,800 psi. Barrels proofed this way were marked either with the crown over N mark or with the crown over Nitro mark. This mark was applied to the flats and to the receiver. The same mark was used on rifled barrels after they passed proof with the above-mentioned powder. In addition, rifled barrels were also marked with a stamp indicating the type of bullet used: St means steel-jacketed bullet, Km refers to a copper-jacketed bullet, while Bl refers to a lead bullet. Also indicated was the weight of the bullet, this being marked in grams and 1/10th grams.

7,9
57
2,4g BlP
N St.m 12,7g

indicates the caliber (7,9 or 8 mm), the length of the cartridge case, in this instance 57 mm.

A Model 88 8 mm rifle, if proofed with a 226.8 grain steel-jacketed bullet would have these marks: Crown over N for semi-smokeless proof; 8 mm / 57 to identify the caliber (it should be noted that the 8 mm is often marked as either 7,99 mm or even as 7,8 mm), and the 57 again refers to the cartridge case length. Finally, there will be St. M. G. / 14,7 g indicating type and weight of the bullet. The proof house at Zella-Mehlis also added month and year of proof—4.12, for example, refers to April 1912.

This was the time that German cartridge cases were standardized, and one of the first calibers to be standardized was the old 9.3x72, today known as the 9.3x72 R. The 9.3x72 was then known under a multitude of names and designations, all of them very much alike. The confusion about this caliber was then cleared up by naming the cartridge the 9.3x71 Normal. This new round required only a minor magazine alteration, and the 9.3x71 Normal chambers in all other 9.3x72 rifles. To facilitate this change-over to the new caliber, it was decided that guns with an altered magazine for the new round would not have to undergo proof again. A shooter with a rifle that had been changed for the 9.3x71 Normal could, without endangering himself or his rifle, fire the old cartridges in his gun.

Shotgun barrels proofed for black powder from then on were marked only with crown over eagle  as well as the caliber stamp 

.

This system worked out so well that it was retained until the proof law of 1939 became effective. The only other changes were in the cartridge designations which were changed between 1912 and 1913, and the addition of the letter "R" indicating a rimmed case.

THE PROOF LAW OF 1939

This law proved satisfactory not only for the shooter and hunter, but also for the gunsmith and the gun trade in general. The most important point is the disappearance of the black powder proof for all firearms for which semi-smokeless ammunition is available. Hand in hand with this came also the withdrawal of recognition of all foreign black powder proofs.

The new law was published on June 7, 1939, and the conditions and rules for proof made their first appearance on July 8 of that year. The law became effective on April 1, 1940 in Germany and on June 1 in Austria and the Sudeten Protectorate. On July 23 of that year, a decree was issued which recognized the Prague proof marks as acceptable within the framework of the new German proof law.

In addition to the proof law itself, there were numerous decrees and orders issued, and the most important of those are: The method of proof, rules concerning chamber dimensions, groove diameter, chamber pressure tables for rifle cartridges and tables of proof loads for smoothbored barrels.

The new proof law appeared in the Reich Law Bulletin *(Reichsgesetzblatt)* No. 126 on July 15, 1939 and reaffirmed the old concept that no small arm which has not been proofed by a state-recognized proof house can be brought into general commerce in firearms and cannot be sold if it does not bear appropriate proof marks. Each firearm that has passed proof firing must be marked with the suitable mark or stamp. The new proof law calls for marking of all important parts of a gun that underwent proof firing, and parts of the gun to be proofed separately must be marked with the appropriate stamp after passing the tests.

Small arms are defined as all such firearms, with short or long barrel, which are capable of discharging a projectile which may be shot, a single bullet, fireworks, gas or other type of projectiles. Excluded are the blank cartridge arms which can only fire a blank cartridge without a bullet or projectile. Also excluded are firearms chambered for gallery or target cartridges *(Zimmerstützenpatronen)* and also excluded are all collector's guns and those used only for scientific purposes, this would include, for instance, the tranquilizer guns.

As important parts of a firearm, the law considers: Interchangeable and finished barrels; locks and breech locks; cylinders serving as chamber, as in revolvers. Such parts which allow quick interchange of parts without tools are considered as interchangeable. On interchangeable parts of the action, those parts involved in the proper closure of the action, as well as parts of selfloading firearms which are essential for the proper functioning of the gun, as well as slide return stop and other such devices, are considered under the new law as essential parts. Such parts, assembled in the gun, are marked with the proof stamp after final proof is completed.

All proofing of firearms must take place at an official proof house or a branch office. Proof houses exist in Oberndorf am Neckar, Suhl and Zella-Mehlis. The proof house at Frankfurt an der Oder was closed, and after June 1, 1940, the proof houses of Ferlach, Weipert and Vienna were added to the list of German proof houses. Each of the proof facilities has its own proof mark, and each gun proofed at a specific facility must be stamped with the identifying mark of that proof house. The following proof houses and marks are being used:

Oberndorf a. N.:	Stag's Antler or Horn (see under 1952, ULM).
Zella-Mehlis:	Heart with fir tree. Author was unable to secure a sample of this mark.
Suhl:	Sole with ax or pick (see 1950).
Ferlach:	Escutcheon of Carinthia (see under Austria).
Vienna:	A cross within an escutcheon (see under Austria).
Weipert:	A falling fir tree within the escutcheon, above it two iron clubs or flails (see under Austria).

The marks assigned to the branch proof houses were to be assigned by the Minister of Economics. However, the branch facilities were never opened, with the possible exception of Steyr which long has been a branch of the Vienna proof house (see under Austria). The Steyr facilities used the Vienna mark.

Small arms or parts for such guns, which are being submitted for proof must be delivered with the proper legal forms filled out, and shipping charges to the proof house must be prepaid. For individuals living abroad, the proof house personnel may make an exception and fill out the required forms after the gun to be proofed has been received at the proof facilities.

The following information must be contained on the delivery slip to the proof house:

a) Address of person submitting gun for proof;
b) Type of cartridge or shell for which gun is chambered;
c) If maximum permissible chamber pressure for the gun submitted is not known, the chamber pressure developed by the shell or cartridge to be used which is to be the basis for proof must be submitted. On demand by the proof master, the person requesting proof must also furnish, in writing, the load data, including type and weight of powder charge, type, length and weight of projectile;
d) In case of repaired or altered guns, the exact nature of the work done must be explained in writing;
e) If the gun was made abroad, or assembled in Germany from parts made abroad, name and location of factory and country of origin must be given. In the case of guns assembled in Germany, name and location of the assembling plant or gun maker must be supplied.

After World War II, this last point was important since manufacture of rifled barrels was forbidden in Germany, and barrels had to be imported.

Upon delivery of a gun to a proof house or branch proof facility, the person submitting the gun for proof may request that the gun be tested with a load that exceeds the pressure levels developed by the standard proof load; this type of proof is known as re-enforced or intensified proof *(verstärkter Beschuß)*.

If there is any doubt, the proof house authorities may request proof that the maker or repairer of the gun is licensed to manufacture or repair small arms. If the domestic origin of a gun is questionable, the proof authorities may request documentation of the maker's manufacturing plant and plant site.

Prior to proofing, the proof house must ascertain if any of these external faults or failures exist:

a) By visual inspection, if the material is free of structural faults, and that cosmetic faults do not affect performance;
b) If barrel joints in multi-barrel guns are free of faults or damages;
c) If action, breech or lock function properly and if, in case of double-barrel guns, the barrels lock up tight with the standing breech;
d) If firing pins or strikers move easily, do not protrude from the bolt face or the face of the standing breech, that there are no burrs at the point of the firing pin, that the firing pin hole is free of burrs;
e) If in magazine guns and selfloading firearms, the feeding and ejecting cycle functions flawlessly, that a round of ammunition can be inserted into a magazine and chambered without difficulties, and that the safety lever works reliably during the loading-shooting cycle;
f) If in revolvers, the gun indexes properly, the cylinder is finished inside and out, and the chambers are clean and well polished.

For small arms for which chamber dimensions have been determined, the bore diameter and chamber dimensions must be determined prior to final proof, and these must agree with the established standards.

Prior to final proof of smoothbored and rifled barrels, the fit of the submitted ammunition into the chamber must be checked, if the ammunition measurements agree with the specified chamber dimensions, and if the chamber is in a straight line with the barrel and action. The maximum dimensional dummy round with the heaviest and largest bullet should chamber without forcing or feel.

All types of small arms undergo final or definitive proof. With some types of firearms, the final proof must be preceded by a first proof of the barrel or barrels in the white, and this proof is designed to test the strength of the material used in the barrel. For this proof, barrels must be completely finished and polished outside; the inside of the barrel must be smooth and polished; and the barrel must be supplied with a breech plug or screw which has a flash hole or vent no larger than .063 inch. The rear section of the barrel must be finished to such a degree that any later work on that section of the barrel will not weaken the barrel walls.

As first proof, a load of black powder is used, and the intensity or strength of the powder depends on the caliber or gauge being tested. The suitable powders and charges are listed in the appropriate load tables for first proof. After having passed first proof, if such proof is called for, and certainly before the gun undergoes final proof, there is yet another: the second proof. This proof is performed when the firearm is completely finished, and the internal and external dimensions of the barrel meet all the specified requirements. The action and the barrel may still be in the white, or they may be blued.

During this proof, the dimensions of chambers and barrels are verified again, and the gun is checked for the presence of the required maker and caliber marks, and the proof mark of the preceding proof, where prescribed by law, must be clearly visible. Should chamber dimension tables make no mention of the caliber or gauge, then the dimensional requirements for proof are waived. Top-break guns chambered for rimless ammuition fall into this category. The proof master may make an exception at his discretion about this rule. This is especially important for foreign buyers since their ammunition sources may not be able to furnish domestic, that is German, ammunition at all times. The proof law was not written to hamper the work of the gunsmith and make it difficult for him to accept or handle such foreign orders. Most of these firearms are quite costly and high performance demands are placed on them, hence great care is used in the manufacture of such guns and such work is definitely encouraged.

After a gun has passed inspection and first proof, the final or definitive proof is next, and for this, the following rules apply:

a) Smoothbored barrels are tested with one shot using black powder and two nitro powder shots;

b) Centerfire rifle barrels and semiautomatic pistols are tested with two shots using nitro powder;
c) All other guns are proofed with one shot using nitro powder, if commercially produced ammunition loaded with nitro powder is available. If such ammunition is not available, then the gun is proofed with one shot of black powder.

Proof of rifle barrels is to be conducted with proof powder 1847. Should this powder not be able to reach the required chamber pressure, then the State Institute of Chemistry and Technology may permit use of another propellant powder.

If the proof consists of firing two shots from the same chamber, the two shots are to be fired without intervening examination of the gun. For multi-barrel guns, primarily double-barrel guns, one shot is fired in each barrel. Proof is considered incomplete when the chamber pressure does not reach the required level. This rule also applies if during the first proof firing of the barrel, the action or lock work was loosened and the proof master feels that the gun being proofed is faulty. In such instance, the proof master may exceed the number of prescribed proof shots, and depending on circumstances, either standard or proof loads may be used for this testing. Arms which repeatedly fail or which fire a round prematurely must be returned to the person requesting proof without further testing.

The black powder loads are determined by means of load data tables, and 151.2 grains of this powder with 586 grains of No. 3 shot and a felt wad suitable for the gauge of the gun being proofed, must create a pressure level that can be read from the first read-off point on the international pressure system. With a 16 gauge gun, the minimum chamber pressure must be 9956 psi. Proof with nitro powder ammunition is performed least 30 per cent excess chamber pressure over the most powerful black powder or semi-smokeless powder standard cartridge of the same caliber.

The permissible upper limit of the standard chamber pressure is listed in a special table in the new proof law. The shotshells for proof also must create adequate pressure so that the pressure can be seen on the first read-off position, and for 16 gauge must record at least 12,090 psi. The nitro proof is to be performed with special proof loads. Proof loads for rifles must produce at least 30 per cent more pressure than the strongest of the black powder loads or semi-smokeless standard rounds for that caliber. Again, the permissible upper limit of the standard chamber pressure can be found in a special table that accompanies the proof rules.

Proof loads for 16 gauge or larger smoothbored barrels must record at least 11,379 psi on the international gas pressure apparatus at recording point I, but pressure may not exceed 4267 psi at point II of the scale.

Shotguns with chambers longer than 70 mm or 2¾ inch may, at measuring point I, show an increased pressure of 1422 psi for each chamber lentgh increase of 5 mm or .197 inch. This proof, which is comparable to international proof rules, was at the time more than adequate for even the most potent of the commercial shotshells. Since then however, heavier commercial loads measuring 70 mm or 2¾ inch have become available in the United States, and these produce higher pressures which do not necessarily indicate a better performance. In some cases such shotshells produce pressures very near to the proof pressures, so that, if the shooter wants to use such ammunition frequently, he had best submit his gun for re-proof.

In submitting a firearm with rifled barrels for nitro proof, the cartridges submitted with the gun for proof must be listed on the delivery slip. The following ammunition information must be furnished to the proof house: Type and charge of powder, weight and type of bullet, as well as the chamber pressure. On demand of the proof house authorities, any person submitting a gun for proof, must furnish the proof master with suitable cartridge cases and bullets or with complete standard rounds.

The usual trade terminology is to be used in describing ammunition. For rifle cartridges the metric caliber designation must be given, and caliber measurements refer to measuring the bore from groove to groove. Further, any cartridge case description must be added, such as "R" for rimmed, "JS" for the 8x57 and the 8x57R round with S-caliber, that is the smaller or .318 inch 8 mm round which has become illegal since the introduction ot this act. Aside from the marks (name of maker of the barrels and serial number), firearms must also carry these identifying stamps or marks:

a) Small arms must have the caliber designation either in millimeters or the currently used trade designation;
b) Any shotgun or rifle barrels made in Germany, excepting those for smallbore rifles and Flobert rifles, must have the DIN mark, this

indicating the material used in the barrel. DIN (Deutsche Industrie-Norm) is the German Industrial Standard which not only specifies composition of materials, but also size of letterheads, etc.

c) Shotgun barrels must be marked as in b) and also must be marked for gauge or shotshell length;

d) Rifle barrels must carry the stamps noted in b) and also the customary cartridge designation, indicating not only the usual trade description, but also the strongest service round made for this caliber;

e) Flobert rifles are to be marked: Flobert.

The proof mark must be affixed on the barrel and action, but in such a manner as not to mark the appearance or finish. The mark indicating first proof must be stamped so that the mark remains visible and undamaged while further work is performed on the barrel.

On actions, the proof mark should be applied on an area where the barrel breeches against the action. On revolvers, the proof mark is to be applied to the cylinder.

The mark indicating repairs is, in cases of an altered gun part, to be affixed under or next to the existing proof mark. Replacement parts are, however, marked only with the repair stamp. In the case of new guns where the manufacturer for some reason has replaced a part that must undergo proof with another part, the newly installed part must be marked when the gun undergoes proof, and here the application of the proof mark is identical to the system used for new guns.

If the year is to be marked, only the last two digits or numbers of the year are to be used. It is permissible to precede this with the number of the month. Thus, 255 would indicate February 1955.

All guns submitted for proof must have a space which is suitable for the application of the proof marks. If no such space is provided, then the gun must be returned from the proof house without proof marks, to the person submitting the gun. A severe penalty is in store for the maker of such a firearm since in effect it voids the proof testing performed on the arm.

The stamp of the proof house and the year when the proof testing was done are marked only once on multi-barrel guns. If a gun is returned without the proof mark, then only the mark of the proof house is to be applied. In such cases where an already proofed gun or a part fails, the

×. or cancellation mark is to be applied over the proof mark. If, at some later date, the gun is to undergo proof again, such proofing may only be done at the proof house where the gun was proofed previously.

After each proof shot, the gun is to be examined. Should faults be found, thus endangering the strength of the firearm, the gun must be returned without being marked with the proof stamp. If faults are such that repairs cannot be effected without endangering the shooter, such defective gun parts must be destroyed or made useless before being returned.

The following defects fall into this class: bulging of barrel; stretching of the chamber*; cracks or other defects in steel; splintering and other faults, including incompletely finished areas. A visual inspection of barrels with a breech system or mechanism is obligatory after first as well as after final proof.

* In case where there is a stretching of the chambers in top-break guns as well as in other rifle barrels, where the service or standard round develops a chamber pressure in excess of 49,780 psi, as well as in all other firearms, the proof master, at his discretion, may have measurements taken with an inside micrometer at the forward and the rear 1/3 of the chamber. Before and after proof firing, the location where the measurements are taken must be taken with reference to a fixed point, such as the end of the barrel, a milled cut in the receiver, etc. To determine areas which are out of round, two measurements are to be taken with a micrometer, the measurements being at a 90 degree angle to each other. The stretching of the action (d) can be calculated with the help of this formula:

$$d \quad L\frac{P1 - P2}{P}$$

where: L is the difference between the internal diameters of the measurements before and after proof firing,
P is the length of the chamber,
P1 is the forward diameter and
P2 the rear diameter of the chamber.

After publication of the German Industry Standards, especially those concerning barrel steels, the proof master may, after barrel material specifications and chamber wall thickness data have been published, waive examination of circumferential stretching of chambers. However, this rule does not apply to top-break guns. Should chamber expansion or stretching exceed 0.2 per cent, the gun must be considered as not having passed proof.

1) Such visual inspection must include all autoloading guns as well as all other guns containing more than one round of ammunition. It must be determined if the ammunition moved freely from magazine to chamber, if the guns's mechanism functioned flawlessly, if the ammunition did not jam up and if ignition was regular and reliable.
2) In long guns
   a) If there was stretching of the chamber;
   b) If primary extraction was accomplished easily;
   c) If the chamber dimensions corresponded with those of the cartridge;
   d) On multi-barrel guns, it must be ascertained that the joints between barrels are perfect and undamaged;
   e) If any changes occured in the action, such as stretching, cracks, swelling etc.
3) In short-barreled guns, such as revolvers, it must be ascertained that cylinder rotation and indexing are perfect. Chambers must be smooth and polished, there shall be no fissures, cracks or other visual imperfections or stretching of the cylinder. If the need aries, deformation of chambers and lock system, not visible to the unaided eye, must be checked with dummy rounds, including cylinder gap.

A proof master may return a gun without proof marks, even if the gun passed all proofs, when visual inspection reveals faults which could endanger the physical welfare of the shooter firing the gun. At the proof master's discretion, such a gun may be made unserviceable before being returned to the owner. In case a gun is returned, either the gun or the faulty parts must be marked. This is one of the best features of the 1939 proof law since it effectively protects all shooters and hunters.

The proof marks of 1939 are compared, at the end of this chapter with those in effect following the proof law of 1891.

Whoever either repairs or undertakes major alterations on parts must submit the gun for another definitive proof, known as repair proof *(Instandsetzungsbeschuß)*. The following alterations or repairs performed on a firearm make the gun liable for repair proof: Changes of barrel or internal changes, changes on the action including the bolt, changes in the chambers of a revolver cylinder, installation of telescopic sights, or any other such work. Any cuts or milling operations on the barrel or other vital parts of the gun also call for re-proof. In the repair proof, the general rules of final or definitive proof apply.

If on multi-barrel guns only one barrel was altered or replaced without affecting the other barrel or barrels, the re-proof may be limited to that repaired or altered barrel. However, if the rest of the barrels were not proofed with nitro powder, or the existing proof marks do not indicate final proof, then all of the barrels must undergo the final proof.

Repair re-proof is not necessary if a part, already proofed and bearing the proper mark, was installed, of if the repairs are of minor external damages, including refinishing.

Certain changes or repairs are prohibited. Arms which are repaired or changed despite the law, or guns which were assembled from other guns or parts, may not be proofed, but may be confiscated by the proof house. Included are welding jobs on barrels, ribs, covers of actions such as dust covers, or any change by welding in the chamber; in top-break guns, no welds are permitted on the hinge tang or any other important part. Such firearms will not be admitted to proof. Welding is defined as any heating which can affect the strength of the barrel steel and hence endanger its future performance.

Lining of barrels and chambers is permitted only for firearms chambered for the .22 caliber rimfire cartridges. This ruling was long overdue, and no conscientious gunsmith would attempt such an undertaking, but sad to report, it has taken place with dire results.

The law empowers the Minister of Economics, in conjunction with the Minister of Domestic Affairs, ro require that guns which are out of proof thanks to a time lapse, must be fully re-proofed. On closer study, this condition is self-explanatory since the duration of effective proof is self-limiting, even if such factors as metal fatigue and stress, introduction of new and hotter powders, as well as changes in factory loadings, are taken into consideration. Old guns and new powders make any old proof, and therefore the safety of the gun, highly speculative.

It should be noted here that all of the European proof laws fall short of knowledgeable reasoning in this aspect of proof law and changes in propellants. The new German proof law was the first to point out this shortcoming, but even this rule was never implemented since nobody ever got around to determining the duration of proof, or a time span when such a gun should be submitted to voluntary re-proof. Even in Austria the new proof law falls short here, although the writers of this law borrowed liberally from the German proof laws. No provisions are made for voluntary re-proof or for a time span during which proof can be considered to be valid. English laws regarding proof, though quite explicit, do not cover this point either, and the proof authorities are content with an appeal to gunsmith and gun owner regarding voluntary re-proof. New proof regulations may, eventually specify period of proof, but as of the moment, no definite rulings have been issued.

Such rules are of special importance, notably in Great Britain, where many smoothbores are so weak near the muzzle that they cannot withstand a load of one ounce of shot in a 12 gauge, nor can they withstand the pressure created by normal loads with progressively burning powders. However, many of these guns, with fast burning powder charges, easily withstood proof, especially in the chamber section of the barrel or barrels.

Excluded from the new proof law—and this is the case with nearly all such laws everywhere—are weapons made for the military services, or guns repaired or in any way altered or changed for military use exclusively. This means that any such guns, when they become surplus and are being readied for sale to shooters and collectors, must undergo re-proof.

This provision of the proof law is important to all those collectors and hunters who own such guns, and this of course includes all those military rifles which have been sporterized. Forgetting about the proof law or not knowing about this section of it is no excuse in court!

Guns made abroad and bearing the appropriate proof marks are not required to be re-proofed. The agreement of July 15, 1914, between Germany, Belgium, France and Italy, calls for mutual recognition of each other's proof rules. Since this agreement became effective, only those proof marks are recognized which indicate proof with semi-smokeless powder. Since 1914, Austria and Spain have joined this agreement, and those marks are acceptable now in Germany. Although Hungary joined too, there seems to be some question among German proof masters whether the Hungarian marks are wholly acceptable. Until the take-over of Czechoslovakia in 1940, the Czech marks were not recognized as valid in Germany, and here too the question remains whether after 1945, the Czech proof is recognized by the German proof houses. Through a series of special agreements, the British proof law has been recognized here, and the German proof has been reciprocally accepted in Great Britain. However, on May 22, 1946, Great Britain cancelled that agreement, and as of this moment, no reciprocal proof agreement exists between Great Britain and West Germany.

Just what the status of proof acceptance is between West Germany and some of the countries which were enemies during World War II is uncertain. West German proof authorities were relvetant to comment on the acceptance of German proof marks abroad, or those from other countries by West German proof masters.

The proof law of 1939 clearly states that ammunition for small arms, and here the law is concerned only with non-military firearms, must meet dimensional standards, must be suitably marked with the name of the maker, and all the needed information about the ammunition as well as the maker's name must appear on the package as it is sold in the trade. Exempt from this rule is military ammunition which was manufactured for the military service of West Germany.

Firearms and other shooting devices which, according to the proof law of 1939 need not undergo proof, must be proofed if the owner so requests and the proof office can accomodate such requests.

The rules to be observed by those submitting arms and ammunition to the proof house are as follows:

Cartridges for rifles must be submitted in the sealed factory package, the same way they are found in the trade. The package must be sealed with a long-lasting sealant, and the package itself may not show traces of having been tampered with or having been opened. The glued label used for this purpose must show the name of the ammunition factory as well as the customary trade designation of the ammunition, such as 8x57 R. Exempt from this rule is ammunition that is used exclusively on an accredited police range.

Brand name ammunition must bear the name of the concern selling this ammunition and under the law, the seller of such ammunition is considered as ammunition manufacturer. Since the seller therefore assumes the responsibility for the ammunition, he must also comply with all points of the law.

Rifle cartridges producing a chamber pressure in excess of that specified in the proof tables, and shotshells creating chamber pressures 75 per cent in excess of the permissible proof chamber pressure, may only be

traded or left to someone if they are contained in the original and completely sealed factory package. Such packages must also bear the legend on the sealing label:
„ACHTUNG! In normalgeprüften Waffen nicht verwendbar!"
"Caution! This Ammunition Is Not To Be used In Guns with Standard Proof."

Each such cartridge or shell must further be indentified by having a serration on the rim of the case or shell casing.

This ruling therefore includes the American cartridges known here as "Heavies" and compliance with the law is recommended since some of the older rifles, when fired with these modern cartridges, may not be safe, thus presenting a serious danger for the shooter.

Cartridges manufactured in Germany and made for export only need not comply with the rules.

The pressure for a cartridge as recorded in the tables is the mathematical median of at least 10 consecutive pressure tests. These tests must come from one production run, and the system used to determine pressure must be one that is acceptable to the proof authorities and to the government. A deviation of the maximum pressure from the standard pressure can be disregarded as long as the maximum pressure does not exceed the standard pressure levels by 15 per cent.

Penalties for breaking the law are quite specific, and can either be in the from of a fine or a prison term up to six months. Aside from the penalty, the gun and ammunition can be confiscated, eveh if they are not the property of the person convicted of the crime. If no person can be prosecuted for the breaking of the law, and a definite violation exists, the firearm and/or ammunition can be confiscated.

Some rules regarding atique guns and shooting devices of historic interest follow. However, since the proof rules have largely been changed since the law of 1939 went into effect, they are no longer applicable.

In the year of 1945, the manufacture or use of any firearm was prohibited in Germany. However, as early as 1948, manufacture of shotguns was resumed in Suhl which was then, and still is, in the Russian zone. The proof law of 1939 was used in the proofing of these guns, and only the proof mark was changed. For some time the final or definitive proof mark for black powder was used on all shotguns—sole with ax and the letters SP above it—even though the guns were designed for semi-smokeless powder. According to the proof master, this was done since no semi-smokeless powders were available for testing. On the whole, it has been suggested that such guns be submitted for semi-smokeless re-proof and that the suitable proof marks be applied at that time.

Not until 1952 was the manufacture of firearms permitted in West Germany, and then only on a somewhat limited basis. A proof house was established in Ulm which is, in essence, the successor to the proof facilities at Oberndorf am Neckar, and therefore the antlers or stag horn mark is now being used by the Ulm proof house. The proof law of 1939 has been retained and only the proof marks have been changed.

SUMMARY

Every German shotgun in good condition can be fired safely with the suitable shell of correct length loaded with semi-smokeless powder, if the gun is marked with a crown over N stamp or crown over Nitro. Shotguns proofed after 1912, if they are to be used with shells measuring 2 3/4 inch (70 mm), must carry the number "70" on the barrel and chamber. If a gun does not carry this designation, then it is chambered for 2 1/2 inch (65 mm) shells, and the longer shells should not be used in such a shotgun.

Firing short shells in long chambers with limited forcing cone is not recommended. It is best if the chamber and shell dimensions are identical, or if there is a long forcing cone. It must be understood that this limits the performance of the shot as well as enlarging the pattern. If a shotgun is used in this manner, great care must be taken that the forcing cone and chamber are cleaned thoroughly and completely.

For instance, the use of a shorter shell in the right barrel for clay pigeon shooters is acceptable since recoil will be less and, as in skeet, ranges may be shorter.

A shotgun with 2 3/4 inch chambers and an American shell containing over 55.5 grains or 1 1/4 ounces of shot for a 12 gauge gun or a 1 ounce load for a 16 gauge gun—shot load data are clearly marked on American shells—should not be used, except in those instance where guns have undergone special proof. Shotguns not proofed for loads producing 75 per cent excess pressure over and above the normal proof pressure should not be used to fire such shells. This not so much a question of a heavy shot load—many German shotshells prior to World

War II contained over 570 grains or 1.3 ounces of shot—but of the peculiarly high chamber pressure produced by the American propellant powders.

The better quality German shotguns will withstand those higher chamber pressure without trouble, but foresight is better than hindsight!

With rifles, especially those of rather uncertain ancestry, special care must be exercised to use the correct diameter bullet, powder charge and a cartridge case of the correct length. If in doubt, consult an experienced gunsmith. The assumption that, just because a round can be chambered, it is the correct cartridge for the gun is erroneous and more often than not, it will result in a burst rifle and possible injury.

GERMAN PROOF MARKS SINCE 1891

1891	1912[1]	1939	1950	1952
V	—	—	—	—

The "In Stock" or *Vorratszeichen* applied to all guns in hands of dealers when proof law of 1891 became effective.

First preliminary proof of the unfinished barrel. Since 1939 this proof is known as preliminary or material proof.

Second or final black powder proof. Valid only when together with the next mark, that is crown over U, from 1891–1939. Since 1939 only applied to guns for which semi-smokeless ammunition is not available in the open trade.

U	idem	—	—	—

Proof mark with eagle or crown, or with crown alone, seen on firearms as final or definitve proof, also on guns proofed in the finished state, and then marked with crown over B stamp. This mark has not been in use since the proof law of 1939 became effective.

(crown) idem — — —

Proof mark for revolvers and muzzleloading pistols. The crown over U mark must also be applied.

(crown) B — idem — —

This is the proof mark applied to a gun that has undergone proof in the finished condition. Crown over U mark must also be present.

(crown) S — idem — —

Proof mark applied to smoothbored barrels.

(crown) W — idem — —

Proof mark found on choked barrels.

(crown) G — idem — —

Proof mark for rifled barrels.

(crown) SWS — idem — —

Proof mark for choke-bored rifle barrels.

(crown) E — idem — —

Proof mark for express rifle barrels.

(12) — idem idem idem

Gauge designation for breech-loading smoothbore guns.

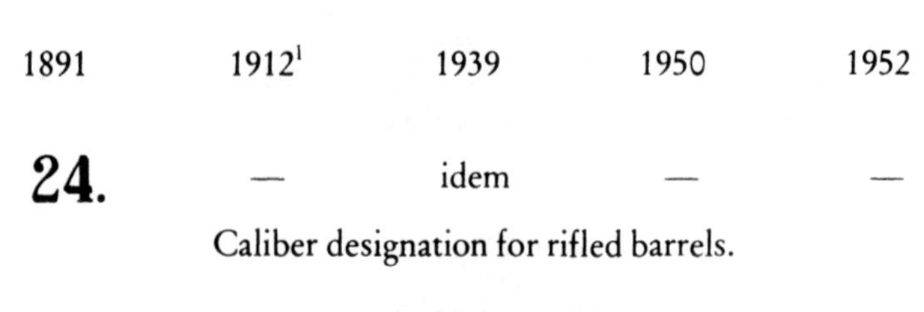

1891	1912[1]	1939	1950	1952
24.	—	idem	—	—

Caliber designation for rifled barrels.

	—		—	

Mark designating new proof after repair.

12g NGPM 71 / 60 g Bl	—	—	—	—

This mark was used for muzzleloading pistols or guns requiring special loads and indicates the load used for proof.

12 g Sch P / 70 g Bl	—	—	—	—
2,2 g Sch P / 32 g Bl	—	—	—	—

This proof mark designated a voluntary proof with a different type of powder than called for in proof regulations. Most of these proofs were performed with the semi-smokeless Schultze powder. Later, only the load data for the standard round for which the gun was proofed were indicated that way.

—				

Proof mark used for the general semi-smokeless proof.

N 2,67 g GBP / St m G	—	—	—	—

Proof mark for smokeless powder proof for rifled barrel with a steel jacketed bullet, in use since July 23, 1893. The "GPB" indicates a special military flake powder *(Gewehr Blättchenpulver)* which, with 41.2 grains (2.67 Gm.), produces 58,800 psi with the indicated bullet.

1891	1912[1]	1939	1950	1952
—	N oder Nitro St m G 12 g	—	—	—

Semi-smokeless proof mark for rifled barrels and steel jacketed bullet. Crown over N or Nitro and the weight of the bullet are listed (in Gm.).

1891	1912[1]	1939	1950	1952
—	N oder Nitro K m G 12,7 g	—	—	—

Same usage, but for copper jacketed bullets.

1891	1912[1]	1939	1950	1952
—	N oder Nitro Bl G 14 g	—	—	—

Same usage, but for lead bullets.

1891	1912[1]	1939	1950	1952
—	8 caliber & chamber 57 length		—	—

The caliber and case length is given in mm.

1891	1912[1]	1939	1950	1952
—	—	 FB	—	 FB

Proof mark for voluntary proof for shoulder and handguns which are not normally subject to proof.

Proof Mark of the Ferlach Proof House[2]

See under Austria

Proof Mark of the Proof House at Frankfurt an der Oder

1891	1912[1]	1939	1950	1952
—	—	Since 1939 no longer in use		

Proof Mark of the Proof House at Oberndorf am Neckar

1891	1912[1]	1939	1950	1952
—	—	See Ulm	—	—

Proof Mark of the Proof House at Suhl

1891	1912[1]	1939	1950	1952
—	—		 15 DR L	—

Proof Mark of the Proof House at Ulm

1891	1912[1]	1939	1950	1952
—	—	—	—	

Proof of the Proof House at Weipert[2]

See under Austria

Proof Mark of the Proof House at Vienna[2]

See under Austria

Proof Mark of the Proof House at Zella-Mehlis

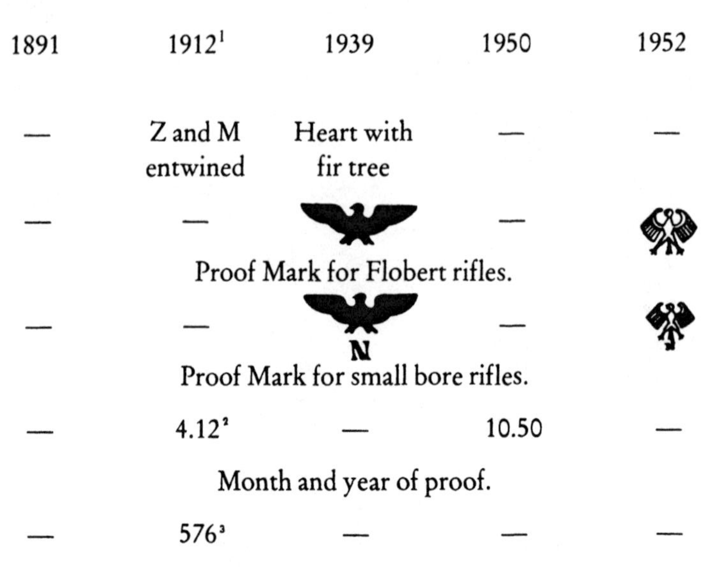

1891	1912[1]	1939	1950	1952
—	Z and M entwined	Heart with fir tree	—	—
—	—		—	
Proof Mark for Flobert rifles.				
—	—	N	—	
Proof Mark for small bore rifles.				
—	4.12[2]	—	10.50	—
Month and year of proof.				
—	576[3]	—	—	—
Number under which gun is listed in proof records.				

Aside from these marks, guns must also be marked thusly since 1939: Handguns must be marked with the caliber in millimeters or with the traditional trade designation.

All domestically produced long barrels, excepting small bore and Flobert, must carry the DIN designation of the barrel.

Flobert barrels must be designated "Flobert."

Shotgun barrels must carry the above-mentioned gauge and chamber length markings.

Rifle barrels must carry the above-mentioned caliber designation or trade markings for the strongest commercially produced cartridge.

---

1 Zella-Mehlis since September 1, 1911; Suhl since April 1912. The proof facilities of Frankfurt a. d. O. used Troisdorfer powder.

2 The proof houses of Vienna, Weipert and Ferlach used this mark from June 1, 1940 until 1945.

3 Date of proof and record number were used at Zella-Mehlis only since October 1, 1911, were discontinued in 1939.

PROOF MARKS OF THE ULM PROOF HOUSE

First proof with black powder, shotguns and multi-barrel rifles.

Final or definitive proof with black powder.

Definitive proof with nitro powder, shotguns, rifles and multi-barrel guns.

Voluntary proof.

Repair proof without renovation or replacement of barrel or action.

Repair proof with renovation or replacement of barrel or action.

Flobert rifles.

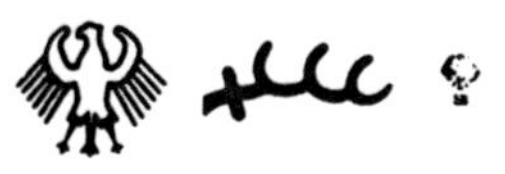

Special purpose guns such as signal and flare guns; gas, stun and blank guns, shooting devices for killing or stunning cattle and the like.

WEST GERMANY

Since 1952 a new proof facility was established at Eckernförde where the factory Sauer & Sohn settled after leaving Suhl. This proof house uses as house mark and the rest of the marks or stamps are identical to those used by the other proof houses. This new proof establishment performs all proofs now in effect in West Germany.

In 1953 yet another proof house, this one in Hannover, was opened for limited service. Until April 21, 1955, the only arms proofed here were small caliber rifles and Flobert guns. It is hoped that in the not too distant future, in conjunction with the State Institute for Physics and Technology in Braunschweig, all other rifle calibers, shotguns and even handguns can be tested. This proof house uses the eagle with N for small bore guns, and without letter for Flobert rifles. As identification, the Hannover proof establishment uses the jumping horse of Saxony 

It should be noted this mark is quite similar to the Colt trademark.

In 1961 the special proof mark for "special purpose handguns" was changed, and underneath the eagle now appears the letter "S" *(Sonderwaffe)* or special weapon.

In 1968 a new Federal gun law became effective. Simultaneously with the gun law, new proof laws were promulgated. The new gun law still calls for proof of every gun produced commercially, whether imported or brought into the country by other means. Guns either repaired or with replacement parts must still undergo proof.

New in this proof regulation are a number of exemptions from proof. For instance, barrel inserts for shotguns as well as barrel inserts for rifled barrels are exempt, providing the gas pressure of the cartridge for the insert barrel does not exceed the pressure produced by the cartridge for which the other barrel is chambered. Also exempt from proof are stud drivers, power actuated tools and stun guns—all of these only undergo construction proof tests.

For gas and scare and blank cartridge guns, proof depends on the caliber. Completely exempt are guns with a chamber diameter no bigger than .236 inch (6 mm) and a chamber length no longer than 6 mm. The greatest difference from the 1939 proof law that can be found is that the small arms to be exported to countries not members of the International Congress of Proof need not undergo proof. This is rather sursprising since the original idea behind the proof laws was to show current and prospective importers that the quality of German arms was superior and that the State saw to it that manufactures maintained a uniformly high standard.

The gun and proof law of 1968 foregoes quality control completely. In proofing a gun, only the following points are considered: Marking each gun with maker's name, safety in operation, functioning, chamber and barrel specifications, and strength and resistance to wear.

1. Markings

Each gun submitted for proof must carry the legally prescribed marks. These consist of:

a) Serial numbers running consecutively;
b) Caliber or gauge designation which must be comprehensive and complete, thus leaving no areas of question or doubt;
d) Name of dealer or maker, if the gun is inported the name or known trademark, including that of the importer in Germany.

2. Dimensional Rules

Examined are all those dimensions which, when either too small or too large, could endanger the user of the firearm. These dimensions are clearly set forth for each caliber and gauge in the law.

a) Minimal dimensions of land and groove measurements for rifled barrels;
b) Minimum chamber dimensions for rifled barrels;
c) Minimum and maximum headspace for all guns;
d) Minimum throat in rifled barrels;
e) Minimum barrel diameter in smoothbored barrels;
f) Minimum and maximum chamber dimensions of smoothbored barrels.

The new law eased many of the strict requirements for gun makers since the maximum dimensions are not given for points a, b, d and e. For point "e" there is another exception since the manufacturer may go below the minimal barrel diameter, providing the gun is submitted to extra strong proof and the actual barrel diameter is clearly marked on the barrel.

Thanks to the new law, commonly referred to as the *BWaffG (Bundeswaffen-Gesetz)* –headspace requirements were reduced by 0.002–0.004 inch.

3. Firearm Handling Safety

Every firearm submitted for proof must be "safe to handle," that is the loading, handling and firing of that firearm may not endanger the shooter.

This presupposes a functioning safety device, a trigger pull that is not too light, nor a trigger so adjusted that simply by closing the action the round in the chamber will fire. In the case of guns with more than one barrel, firing one barrel shall not activate the firing mechanism thanks to recoil and thus discharge the other barrel or barrels. Doubling is dangerous and cannot be permitted on any gun.

4. Strength of Firearms

The strength of all guns is tested with cartridges developing carefully detemined excess chamber pressure, so-called *Beschußpatronen* or proof loads. The BWaffG also specifies that all guns be proofed with nitro or smokeless powder, the black powder proof having been eliminated completely. Also gone is the preliminary proof of semi-finished barrels. The new barrel steels and vastly improved manufacturing methods have made this step possible.

We now differentiate between "normal" and "forced" or intensified proof. In normal proofing, a proof load with a smokeless powder charge is used, and the chamber pressure produced by this load may be 30 per cent above the pressure level produced by the strongest standard round. Guns proofed this way were marked with eagle over N, and the N here no longer means nitro but now means "normal" in contrast to forced proof. According to the new proof law, the nitro proof is compulsory anyhow, hence there is no need to indicate the use of smokeless powder in proofing.

Shotguns designed to fire the magnum shotshells must undergo the forced proof. This includes guns chambered for the 12 gauge 3 inch shell, the 20 gauge 3 inch shell and other such loads. Also included are those shotguns on which bore diameter is less than that prescribed by law for that gauge. The proof pressures for the forced proof for shotguns averages about 50 per cent above that of the chamber pressure created by the strongest standard or commercial round for that gauge.

A forced proof for rifled barrels is available, but only on a voluntary basis. Here the person submitting a gun for proof can specify just how much pressure over the standard round he desires the gun to be proofed for. Such barrels are marked with the gas pressure which the gun withstood during proof firing. On smoothbored barrels, the word "Magnum" is stamped into the steel, directly following the gauge marking. All guns which have passed forced proof are marked with the eagle over V, the V standing for "verstärkt."

Long guns with rifled barrels and semiautomatic pistols are proofed with two shots per barrel. If the maximum pressure of the standard cartridge is below 36,261 psi (2500 bar), only one proof load is fired.

Revolvers are proofed by firing one proof load in each chamber of the cylinder, regardless of the maximum pressure of the standard round. Shotguns are tested with two different proof loads per barrel. One of these loads must produce a pressure 30 per cent in excess of the standard load in the chamber, and this is designed to test not only the chamber but also the locking system of the gun. The other shell is loaded with a progressive powder, usually black powder, and is designed to test the entire length of the barrel, thanks to a sustained pressure level. This load must develop no less than 7252 psi (500 bar) 6.38 inches (162 mm) from the breech face.

5. Functioning Proof

In the course of this test, the mechanism of the gun is tested during and after the proof shot has been fired. The mechanism must function flawlessly, and this proof is of special importance in selfloading guns. Semiautomatic guns, for which the standard cartridge or shell develops a mean pressure below 36,261 psi (2500 bar), are proofed with one proof load, the second round being a standard or factory load.

Proof Marks

The new proof law of 1968 did away with some of the proof marks introduced in 1950. As superior mark the eagle of the Bundesrepublik Deutschland is still in force. The other marks used are as follows.

Guns which passed proof without trouble are marked with the suitable proof mark. This consists of the eagle placed above the appropriate capital letter, the mark of the proof house where the tests were performed, and the date of proofing. Usually the month of proof is added. If so desired, the numbers may be coded into the letter code, where the numbers 1 to 9 represent the letters "a" to "k."

Should fault be found with a gun, either prior to or after proof, the gun is to be marked with the official rejection stamp which consists of the proof house mark and the month-year date stamp.

Gun parts which are damaged in the course of proof so that they cannot be used or repaired, are marked with the rejection mark, and next to it with a stamp *"UNBRAUCHBAR"* or useless. Defective, useless or burst guns are returned to the owner or the person submitting the gun for proof. Such guns are no longer destroyed by smashing or cutting them.

In June of 1971, the first change in the gun law became effective and the German eagle was replaced by a somewhat stylized eagle.

OFFICIAL MARKS OF PROOF HOUSES AND PROOF MARKS SINCE 1968

PROOF HOUSE MARKS

Ulm	Berlin	Kiel	Hannover	Munich (München)	Cologne (Köln)

German eagle mark prior to June 1971.

N

1. Standard proof for all guns.

J

2. Repair proof after repair or replacement of major gun parts.

V

3. Forced proof.

L

4. Proof for guns with special loads which, instead of cartridges or shell, use another means of firing, including gas. Included here are muzzleloaders, salute cannon, etc.

5. Stylized German eagle mark which became effective in June of 1971. The letter code below the eagle was not changed.

Third German Gun Law Ordinances

The following changes and additions were made in the German gun and proof law on May 10, 1973. These changes were approved by the Parliament (Bundesrat) and by the Minister of the Interior as well as the Minister for Labor and Social Order.

I. Proof

All shoulder and handguns, small mortars, salute cannon, insert barrels and barrels which permit an easy means of attaching them to an action (in essence extra barrels the shooter can install himself, as on autoloading and double-barrel shotguns), must undergo proof. Each must pass proof designed for that type of firearm.

On special request, proof testing may be performed on guns not required to undergo proofing.

Firearms, mortars, cannon, insert barrels and replacement barrels should be returned to the person submitting the item for proof if the item is either still in the white, or if suitable ammunition for testing is not furnished. The ammunition rule may be waived under some circumstances.

Any gun, barrel or part that has undergone final machining, polishing, or any other work that could weaken the part, should be considered to be finished, even though still in the white. In the case of firearms and small mortars, the external parts of the barrel, the chambers, and the lock must be finished and the stock fastened to the gun. Under stock, any device that permits handling and proofing the gun is considered acceptable.

II. Methods of Proofing

A request for proof must be submitted in duplicate, and there are no exceptions made to this rule. In the request, the following information must be furnished:

1) Name and address of person requesting proof;
2) The exact type of proof requested, the serial number of the gun, and also the number under which the gun is classified under paragraphs 13 and 14 in the law;
3) A description of the suitable ammunition, or the load data, including weight of charge and type of powder to be used; also projectile information for the most powerful commercial ammunition available for this caliber; or the composition of the flammable liquid or gaseous propelling agent or mixture of such agents;
4) An indication whether or not an essential part of the firearm was either repaired or replaced;
5) It must be specified if the use of ammunition creating extra high chamber pressure is requested.

The person requesting proof must indicate on whose behalf he is doing so, giving complete name and address of that individual. Furthermore,

1) If his name, his firm's name or the registered trade mark of the firm is involved in the transaction, the gun to be proofed must bear his name, firm name or trademark.
2) In case the arm does not bear those identifying marks, or if the proof is requested by a private individual who imported the item or other-

wise introduced the gun so that it comes under the purview of the law, it must be so indicated on the proof application.

If several arms of the same types are being submitted for proof, application can be made for all of them on the same form.

If a gun failed proof and was rejected, the gun must be resubmitted to the proof facility which rejected it originally.

If firearms or shooting devices which require a special load for proof are aubmitted to a proof house and the proof house cannot secure the needed materials, the proof master may request ammunition, shell casings, powder and primers or priming devices.

If barrel inserts or extra barrels are submitted for proof, the proof authority may request a suitable firearm for use in conjunction with testing the material submitted.

Should it become necessary to perform a requested proof, the proof master may request whatever materials he needs to perform the proof testing.

The proof mark must contain the German State eagle; for the normally required proof using ammunition loaded with smokeless powder and normal gas pressure, a letter die with letter "N" is required.

The letter "L" is to be used when the starting device is initiated by a flammable liquid or gas or a mixture; or if a special propellant load is required, then the letter "L" die is to be used beneath the eagle mark.

Firearms which have to undergo proof after repair or replacement of major parts, must be marked with a letter "J" die, this too to be placed below the German eagle mark.

Guns submitted voluntarily for forced proof must be stamped with a die showing the letter "V."

Guns designed to be fired with black powder are to be marked with the letters "SP" below the German eagle mark.

Also to be marked on the gun is the special mark assigned to the proof house where the tests were conducted, plus a stamp indicating month and year and the first figure indicates the month. Thus, 668 would indicate June of 1968. If so desired, the numbers may be substituted by a letter code, from 0 to 9 with the letters "A" to "K" taking the place of the numbers.

The reject mark must contain the proof house mark and the stamp indicating the year. If the item bears a proof mark, the tipped St. Andrew's cross is to be placed over the proof mark. In instances where the item is of antique or historical value, the mark may be placed next to or below the proof mark. Important parts which cannot be repaired must be marked with the previously mentioned mark "useless."

In case of firearms and short mortars, the proof mark must be placed so that it is legible and readily visible. On other important gun parts a simple identifying mark suffices.

In firearms and mortars where there is a separate chamber or loading chamber, the required marks must also be placed on these chambers. In the case of multi-barrel guns, such a mark must be impressed on each barrel. Revolvers need only be marked once, and then only on the cylinder. A replacement or repair proof mark must be placed on the repaired or replaced part.

If so requested, the proof house must supply a signed and duly authorized proof certificate. This must indicate clearly the type of proof as well as the load data for the proof loads.

This is especially important for collector's guns and antique guns where a proof master may, upon request, issue a certificate that any proofing may either damage or completely destroy said gun, and that therefore no proof was performed. This may also be done in case of cartridge guns for which suitable ammunition is not listed in the law and where substitute ammunition was used.

III. Construction

Firearms, insert barrels, flare guns and those using pyrotechnical projectiles must be proofed and marked accordingly. The proof authority may, under certain circumstances, waive this requirement. This applies to such cases where the user of such a device or a third party knowingly accepts the risk of firing the gun, or if the gun, firearm or device does not present a great hazard under the law. The proof authorities can, under some circumstances, require additional proof if, in the opinion of the proof master, firing the gun or device may be dangerous to the shooter or any third person or bystander.

In accordance with the specific clauses in the law, some shooting devices may be classified as flare guns and ammunition or devices using pyrotechnical projectiles or loads.

Items submitted for proof may not have any signs or other marks on them which could be misleading, especially ammunition and load markings.

IV. Examination of Construction

Persons submitting items for proof must list, aside from name and address, the place where the item to be proofed was manufactured. There must also be a complete description of the item, including whether it is a barrel insert, or uses flare ammunition or pyrotechnical effects. Applicant must also submit a sample of the gun or insert barrel, and suitable ammunition or projectiles. The same ruling applies to gas guns, scare or blank guns and signal guns and these must be accompanied by suitable ammunition or projectiles. In case of flare or pyrotechnical devices, adequate ammunition must be furnished.

All of this material must be accompanied by a cross section drawing or an exploded view, giving not only measurements, but also material specifications. This must be submitted in triplicate and instructions for use, as packed with the item, must be submitted also, the instructions being written in German. For firearms or barrel inserts, ammunition must be specified and must be furnished for proof testing. For other shooting devices, the location of manufacture must also be given, and also the location where spare parts can be obtained in case re-proof is called for.

In case of special devices, the applicant must furnish a suitable sample for tests, or a serially numbered production piece. In case the item to be tested is ammunition for a flare gun or pyrotechnical device, such a device or gun must be furnished. Sectional views and dimensional drawings must be submitted with these samples.

In case there is a question about the material used in such devices and shooting apparatuses, the State Physical-Technical Institute and the Central Office for Accident Prevention of the Trade Union Central Committee shall be called upon. If there is doubt about the materials used, the State Material Testing Institute shall be consulted.

In the case of shooting devices which are permanently installed and cannot be moved, the suitable proof house may, in conjunction with the Accident Prevention Office of the suitable trade union, arrange for the needed proof at the site of the installation.

Methods and systems of proofing may, in some instances, be determined by either the State Physical-Technical Institute or the State Material Testing Institute. All such applications and the answers from the respective offices must be in writing. The proof request must include the name and address of the person or organization, manufacturer or importer requesting the tests. Also included must be all construction details, material specifications and also the complete specifications for the suitable ammunition. Also shown must be the name and complete description of the handgun, the insert barrel, the alarm gun, signal gun, guns firing either gases or other irritants or noxious agents, flare guns designed for flare or ammunition with a pyrotechnical performance. Also included must be the trademark and all other marks to be marked on the gun or device, as well as all product limitations as far as use and anticipated durability go. These must be supported by suitable documentation. Imported products must be submitted with the appropriate proof evidence and the instruction manual must be approved by the proof master.

The device submitted for proof must be serially numbered, marked with the trade mark, and after passing proof must be marked by the proof authority with the suitable acceptance or proof mark. Repaired firing devices must be marked in accordance with the repair section of the proof law. Such repair marks must be applied in such a manner that they cannot be removed by interchanging or removing a part of the device. In case the flare or pyrotechnical ammunition is so small that it cannot be marked readily, the suitable markings must appear on the smallest package available in the trade.

The structural details of any such firing device, as well as any recall or proof failure, must be reported in the respective publications of the institute performing the tests or working with the design or material features of the firing device.

V. Re-proof of Shooting Devices and Short Mortars

The user of any such device or apparatus must re-submit the device for proof every two years to either the maker or his agent. Should any kind of failure occur, the device must be re-submitted for proof immediately. The manufacturer or his agent must determine if there is a product failure and if the device is identical to the construction specified for the item. Included here are also those mortars using a shell case that contains the powder charge. The proof authority may specify re-proof periods, providing no time extension is granted that could endanger a user of the device. If the device passes proof, the proof master must apply the suitable marks.

The proof mark applied must follow the sample in design. The last two numbers, indicating the year, must be contained in the small square, and the number of the quarter of the year must be shown in a corner of the large square, standing on a corner within the circle. If the proof is applied in form of a plaque, the same mark is to be used, but the mark must appear in black on a silver-like background. Such a plaque must be affixed either to the barrel or the action in a permanent manner, and it must be placed so that the quarter of the year in which the test was performed is pointed in the direction of the muzzle.

The agent or manufacturer of any shooting device that has undergone proof must be furnished with a proof certificate that shows where and how the device was proofed, the date of proof, as well as the person actually performing the proofing. Such a certificate of proof must also be issued for any short mortar submitted for proof.

VI. Determining Dimensional Specifications for Long Guns, Barrel Inserts and Interchangeable Barrels, as well as Ammunition

Already determined were the dimensional measurements for cartridges and magazines, chambers, land and groove measurements and bore diameters of long guns, barrel inserts and interchangeable barrels as well as headspace.

Also ascertained were the maximum permissible chamber pressures, the usual trade designation of cartridges which fall under the purview of the law and which are commercially produced.

Ammunition that exceeds the established mean pressure levels for that caliber by no more than 15 per cent or the prescribed energy level by no more than 7 per cent, is considered as acceptable.

The chamber pressure and energy level determinations are to be conducted by means of currently acceptable ballistics methods.

In place of the usual cartridge designation. another method may be employed if this designation has been passed upon and published in the regular bulletin of the State Physical-Technical Institute. The designation must be brought to the attention of the public and the designation must be such that it is not possible to mistake that ammunition for any other ammunition or designation.

Should the packaging of the ammunition be too small to permit stating all of the above specified data, it is sufficient to state the caliber and length of the cartridge case if this is a part of the cartridge designation. If cartridge cases are plated, the above-mentioned dimensional specifications apply only to the cartridge case.

Land and groove dimensions may vary somewhat, as long as the bore diameter remains identical to that set forth for the established land and groove measurements.

VII. Proof Council

The State Minister of Trade is to assemble a Council for Proof. The president of this council is to be designated by the Minister of Trade.

The Council is to consist of, aside from the president, one representative from each of the provincial or state governments under which the proof authority operates; one representative each of the State Material Testing Institute and the State Physical-Technical Institute; one representative of the State Criminal Investigation Department; and one representative each of the German Test and Proof Institute for Hunting and Sporting Arms, the German Norm Committee, and the Central Comittee of the appropriate trade unions; three representatives of arms and ammunition manufactures; one representative each of the makers of shooting devices, the Gunsmith Trade Council and the importers of firearms and ammunition.

The members of the Council for Proof must be experts in firearms or ammunition. The Minister of Trade may invite representatives of provincial and city governments as well as other experts to the meetings of the Council of Proof.

The Minister of Trade is to be guided in the selection of the State Criminal Investigation Department representative by the Minister of Domestic Affairs. The representatives of the provincial government are chosen by the Minister of Trade after the provincial council makes the suitable recommendations. The representatives of the various institutes are to be chosen after being interviewed by the heads of their respective agencies. The representatives of the respective manufactures, importers, and trade unions are to be selected by their respective organizations. The members of the Council of Proof will not receive a renumeration for their work.

VIII. Costs

The administrative costs, the costs for performing the required proof tests as well as other tests and examinations are to be based on the scale established by law. If costs for a specific job are not listed therein, the fee for the work must be established by means of the prevailing wage scales set forth.

Costs are to be determined by means of wage scale for proof as described in the appropriate description for admission to proof. For all special tests and proofs, as well as for proof tests performed for special long guns, barrel inserts, and interchangeable barrels when the propellant is either a flammable liquid or gas mixture, or when exceptions are made for proof, or when proof procedures are not described or do not follow standard procedures, the special wage scale shall be used to determine cost. This rate of payment also prevails when the proof authority has to manufacture the ammunition to be used for proof.

If the proof must be performed away from the official proof house or facilities, travel as well as waiting time must be paid for by the person requesting proof, and special arrangements must be made with the proof authority regarding costs.

The hourly pay scale to be used to determine such special charges are to be based on current pay scales. In May of 1975, with the German Mark worth about 42 U.S. cents, the hourly pay rates varied from about $ 14 per hour for the higher ranking technical personnel to $ 12 for skilled help and about $ 10 per hour for unskilled labor. For fractions of a quarter hour, the hourly rate of pay divided by four is to be used to arrive at the total rate.

Only half the proof fee is to be charged if the product being proofed is not safe for use or fails to meet the dimensional specifications, or if no durability testing was performed.

No charge is to be made if the product is returned without being proofed, or if the item does not carry the required maker's or importer's marks, of if the product submitted obviously will not pass proof firing with the ammunition suitable for that gun and caliber.

For multi-barrel long guns, the appropriate proof fee is to be collected for each barrel tested, but multi-barrel handguns are exempt from this ruling.

If proof firing takes place at the facilities of the person or company requesting proof, the proof fee is reduced by 10 per cent. If a proof applicant also supplies the required technical help and material, the proof fee is further reduced by 15 per cent.

If at least 300 short guns with a barrel length of not more than 60 cm (23.6 in.) or 100 long guns with barrels longer than 60 cm (23.6 in.) are proofed and all guns are of identical type and are chambered for the same cartridge, the proof fee is 95 per cent of the total fee set forth, and if 500 short guns or 200 long guns are proofed simultaneously, the fee is 90 per cent of the established proof fee.

The proof fee is also waived if proof firing is either interrupted because of unforeseen circumstances, or if proof firing has to be postponed through no fault of either the proof house or the proof applicant.

The proof applicant must also pay for the packing material required to return a proofed gun or shooting device; the applicant also must pay for whatever foreign ammunition, or ammunition components and the like are required to complete proof firing.

IX. Penalties, Temporary and Final Rules

Penalties are to be assessed for those who either deliberately or carelessly fail to submit a firearm for re-proof after repairs. Penalties must also be paid by those who fail to submit shooting devices or short mortars for the periodic examination.

Shooting devices in use before this law will become effective, must undergo proof when the new proof law becomes official. This means that the proof law becomes fully effective the day after it is published, and the fee lists become effective 1 January, 1973.

RULES OF PROOF FOR LONG GUNS, SHORT MORTARS, BARREL INSERTS, INTERCHANGEABLE BARRELS, AND PROJECTILES WITH PYROTECHNIC ACTION AND TECHNICAL REQUIREMENTS PERTAINING TO PROOF.

German proof consists essentially of two parts, the firing of the gun or other device being tested with special proof loads, and an examination of the gun or device to ascertain the durability of the product being tested.

The durability of long arms and short mortars which are designed to be fired with a propellant powder must be proofed with a special high pressure load.

The durability of long guns, barrel inserts, interchangeable barrels and other such devices which are normally fired by means of a flammable liquid or gaseous propellant mixture, are to be proofed with a special mixture of such a propellant or propellants, and should this not be practical, the proofing is to be done with a special proof projectile.

This mean chamber pressure developed by proof loads, the special load or the mixture of propellants, must exceed, by 30 per cent, the mean chamber pressure developed by the standard service round or the usual load. If, instead of chamber pressure, the energy of the projectile serves as basis of proof, then the proof ammunition or load, or mixture of propellants must produce an energy level 10 per cent in excess of the standard or mean energy produced by the standard load. In case it is not possible to increase the energy level for the required proof firing, then it becomes permissible to use the original load or propellant mixture to achieve the required results. However, the weight of the projectile must be increased by 10 per cent of the original or standard weight of the projectile.

Durability tests of long guns, barrel inserts, interchangeable barrels, short mortars and the like must be determined by means of one shot. Shotguns are to be tested with two rounds, as are rifles in which the standard service round produces a mean chamber pressure in excess of 2500 bar (approximately 36,261 psi). Two shots are to be used also with barrel inserts and interchangeable barrels.

Selfloading guns, which are not revolvers, are to be tested with two shots, where one shot may be a standard factory load.

The durability of guns where the magazine or ammunition storage system is separated from the barrel must be tested by firing one shot from each of the cartridge storing positions.

In multi-barrel guns, durability is to be tested as prescribed for each individual barrel.

Should these tests determine that the durability of a gun, short mortar, barrel insert or interchangeable barrel is inadequate, the proof firing must be repeated.

In testing shotguns, and shotguns with interchangeable barrels, at least one shot of the two shots fired must be done with a proof load which develops a mean pressure of at least 500 bar (approximately 7348 psi) 6.38 inches from the breech face.

After the test firing, a visual inspection is to be made to see if a barrel burst or cracked, if chamber, magazine, or the locking system shows signs of damages. In multi-barrel guns, the inspection must include the joints between the barrels.

The verification of the dimensional specifications of guns, insert barrel and interchangeable barrels is to be performed in the accepted technical manner.

Short mortars to be fired with ammunition may undergo a limited examination, where the dimension of the actual ammuntion is compared with dimensional data furnished by the manufacturer of the mortar.

The adherence to dimensional specifications of firearms is to be examined prior to proof firing as well as after proof firing. The after-proof examination must pay particular attention to any stretching that may have occured in the barrel, chamber, the action or the locking systems.

If proof loads, either for increased chamber pressure or increased energy levels, are used to proof long guns, short mortars, barrel inserts or interchangeable barrels, then the dimensions of that ammuntion must be used as criteria in checking the dimensional specifications of the arm being tested.

The safety in handling and shooting a firearm must take into consideration:

The ease with which a cartridge chambers and the ease of primary extraction of the fired case.

How smoothly the firing pin or pins move in the firing pin hole, that the firing pin or pins do not protrude from the breech face, and that the tip of the firing pin, the firing pin hole and the breech face be free of burrs.

The safety must function flawlessly, and in the case of repeating selfloading firearms, the loading mechanism must function without malfunctions.

In the case of revolvers, the cylinder must rotate freely and index perfectly.

The durability, handling properties and the conforming of the gun, that is excluding shooting devices and barrel inserts, to the established dimensional norm are to be done on hand of a factory prototype.

In the case of shooting devices, this examination is to be done by means of a prototype. The prototype is also to be used to verify that the proof loads for the device can be fired in an open space and that the projectile attains at least 5.57 ft / lb (7.5 J) energy and that the device is not dangerous to a third person. The durability of such a device, and this includes power-actuated stud drivers, cattle stunners and killers and other such products, must be proofed with proof loads, and up to 10 such rounds may be fired.

Measurements to see if the device meets dimensional norms are to be made in accordance with current technical methods, and the data of the manufacturer are acceptable. In some cases, the dimensional tests may be waived, and the measurements of the ammunition and the data of the maker of the device may be simply compared. It must also be ascertained if the device is capable of being fired.

A shooting device firing a solid projectile cannot be considered safe to handle, or not dangerous to third persons, when:

1) There is no safety lever on the device.
2) The device fires when it is being loaded, unloaded, handed to another person, bumped, dropped, or discharges under any such circumstances.
3) When the device can be fired in the open space without the help or misuse of an auxiliary device, or when it can be fired without mechanical alterations.
4) When the device can be fired without having the barrel pressed against a flat surface with a power that is a least equal to the weight of the device, the power applied being at least 11.2 pounds (50 Newtons).
5) If the device can be fired when the barrel and the surface against which it is being pressed are at a slight angle, thus leading to ricochets of the projectile.
6) If the device is not furnished with a protective shield that effectively prevents chips from the surface being fired at from flying back into the face of the user of the device.

7) If the device creates an excessive amount of discharge sound or recoil which is deemed preventable.

Shooting devices firing a solid projectile with a velocity of less than 328 fps are exempt from the above points 4, 5 and 6. However, a device must be considered as having failed proof if it can be fired in an open space and the user's safety is endangered or the device fails to function after such a shot.

A shooting device using a solid driving rod or rammer which remains on the device and is an inherent part of it, is considered unsafe for the user and any bystander if:

1) There is no provision on the device to catch and retain the solid rod or rammer.
2) If the device fires when it is being loaded, unloaded, handed to another person, bumped, dropped or discharges under any other such circumstances. Of if discharge noise or recoil are deemed excessive and preventable by mechanical means.

A non-movable device is considered unsafe if:

1) It cannot be loaded or unloaded without danger of discharging.
2) It does not have a safety lever which effectively prevents firing the device while it is in use.
3) The device does not meet the dimensional specifications set forth for it.

Proof of Construction

A manufacturer's prototype is to be used for: alarm guns, blank guns, guns firing irritating or noxious gases, solids or liquids, and flare and signal guns, with a chamber not longer nor larger in diameter than 6 mm, must comply with the previously cited durability, safety and dimensional norms.

It is to be ascertained if such guns can be fired with conventional ammunition or by means of muzzleloading with a projectile that exceeds an energy level of 5.5 ft/lb.

The energy that can be imparted to a projectile by means of ammunition designed for the gun's bore diameter and chamber must be measured. The proof ammunition to be used must impart the greatest possible energy to the projectile. If no commercial projectiles of the correct diameter are available, suitable lead projectiles may be used. The length of these may not, however, exceed twice the bore diameter.

The projectile's energy is determined by means of the muzzle velocity and the weight of the projectile. The mathematical mean of 10 such tests is considered to be the energy for that projectile.

The following construction details for guns must be examined:

1) The axis of the chamber and the barrel must be aligned so that more than one-half of the chamber diameter is in line with the barrel, and gas vents must be located so that their angle to each other is at least 30 degrees, or
2) In the barrel or gas vents there must be built-in traps which are integral parts of the gun and cannot be removed readily with any tool readily obtainable on the open market, or similar devices or designs as in 1 and 2 must be incorporated.
3) Guns which can be taken down into their component parts must be tested to ascertain that no single part alone can be used to fire a projectile.

No failure criteria are given for any conversion work performed on the firearm, especially such jobs as altering or enlarging either the chamber or the bore of the barrel.

Gas vents in guns with bore diameter of more than 6 mm may not be covered over, removed or obstructed so that the projectile's kinetic energy cannot exceed 5.5 ft/lb without endangering the user of the gun.

Neither the gun, nor essential parts of it may break or fall apart.

Pyrotechnical ammunition and projectiles with pyrotechnical properties, must meet the following criteria:

1) None of the glues, adhesive materials and other ejecta may contain mechanical impurities.
2) The pyrotechnical components may not give an acid reaction unless neither shelf life nor the safety of the user is endangered.
3) Furthermore, pyrotechnical ammunition may not contain:
   Sulfur with free sulfuric acid, or with more than 0.1 per cent of non-burning particles;
   Free sulfur;
   White or yellow phosphorus;
   Potassium chlorate which contains more than 0.15 per cent bromine.

Flare ammunition and ammunition with pyrotechnical effects must be made in such a fashion that it is safe for its intended use and the pyrotechnical components must be fastened into the shell in such a manner that they cannot fall out and become loose in the case. Such ammunition must also be protected against accidental discharge, preferably by means of a protective cap or special methods of packaging.

Furthermore, the igniter used in flare ammunition and cartridges with pyrotechnical properties must be self-igniting. A four-week storage at 122 F. may not produce any chemical changes, or produce hazardous conditions for the user. If such ammunition with various types of igniters is stored together, such storage must not lead to self-ignition or any chemical reaction with either the component parts of the igniters or the igniters themselves.

Igniters may not contain: Metallic chlorate salts, antimony, sulfides, or potassium hexacyanoferrate. Ammonia salts, or their amines with chlorates, except when incorporated for making smoke devices and shells. In such instances, an adequate shelf life must be provided for.

If any such ammunition contains more than one igniter, care must be taken that no chemical reaction between the igniters can occur which might result in the production of any of the above-cited chemicals. Igniters for flare ammunition and rounds with pyrotechnical properties which contain chlorates may not have a total content of chlorate which exceeds 70 per cent. The barium chlorate base in flare cartridges, as well as the chlorate content in whistling cartridges, may be increased up to 80 per cent.

Flare ammunition is to be classified into Class R 1 if the pyrotechnical igniter and the driving charge does not weigh more than 308.6 grains and the maximum rise is 109.3 yards (100 m). Such ammunition may neither explode, detonate, nor ignite when hit accidentally. During an accidental discharge, the ammunition may not produce particles with sharp edges which could be propelled through the air.

Flare ammunition is to be classified into Class G1 if it does not contain more than 154.3 grains (10 grams) of igniters and does not exceed a maximum rise of 109.3 yards (100 m). Nor should such ammunition be capable of being ignited accidentally by being struck or by being exposed to fire, nor should the regular method of igniting it produce sharp-edged parts which can endanger bystanders, nor can such ammunition contain a sound-producing igniter.

Flare ammunition to be classified in Class G1 must be so designed that the burning rate of the projectiles is such that on firing they attain a kinetic energy 4.4 ft / lb when moving straight up into the air, and they must return to the ground, fully extinguished.

The diameter of flare ammunition and projectiles with pyrotechnical properties must correspond to the bore diameter of the gun or device from which such ammunition is to be fired. The chamber pressure created by such ammunition may not produce a chamber pressure greater than 30 per cent over the pressure produced by projectiles without pyrotechnical charge.
If the proof applicant submits a certificate of either the manufacturer or an appropriate technical research and testing institute, the chemical analysis of the components contained in such ammunition may be waived.

Illustration No. 1  Federal Eagle

Illustration No. 2 Marks of the German Proof Houses

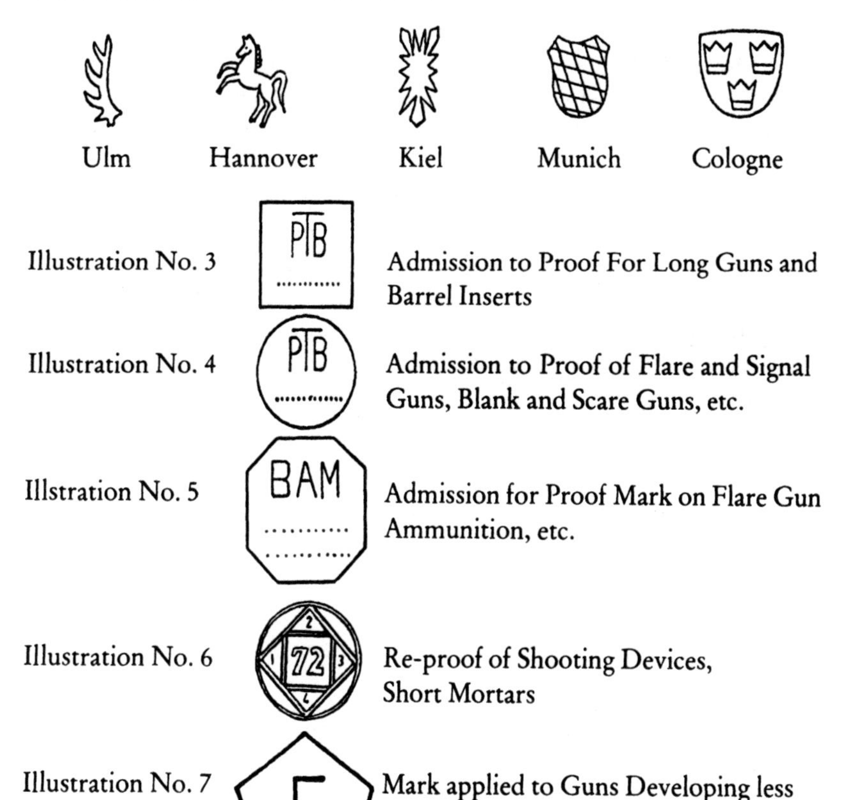

Illustration No. 3 — Admission to Proof For Long Guns and Barrel Inserts

Illustration No. 4 — Admission to Proof of Flare and Signal Guns, Blank and Scare Guns, etc.

Illstration No. 5 — Admission for Proof Mark on Flare Gun Ammunition, etc.

Illustration No. 6 — Re-proof of Shooting Devices, Short Mortars

Illustration No. 7 — Mark applied to Guns Developing less than 5.5 ft/lb Kinetic Energy

EAST GERMANY

Although many of the better known gun companies moved from Suhl after World War II and began anew in West Germany, a great deal of gun finishing went on in Suhl and the surrounding areas at that time. Among the guns finished during this period were many bearing the Merkel and the Simson names.

As basis for the new proof laws, the German proof law of 1939 was used, and even the old Suhl mark, the sole with imbedded ax, was used. The letter "M" mark was added, this indicating the material inspection which takes place prior to the first proof firing. The letters "SP" serve to indicate final proof for black powder guns, and the letter "N" is used to denote final semi-smokeless proof.

To designate the new proof house at Suhl, the letters "DR" within an oval were added. Somewhat later, it was discovered that the new proof house mark was totally unknown outside East Germany and that this lack of recognition would most certainly have an undesired effect on exported sporting arms. Consequently, in 1950, the world-famed Suhl mark was re-introduced, but by now the eagle had been stylized and somewhat streamlined. To prevent possible mixups with older guns, the last two digits of the year as well as the number of the months have been affixed since 1945. This is superposed on the eagle, and the number 1254 indicates December 1954.

The proof house, operating under the Office for Measures and Product Testing and now named Proof Office for Long Guns ("Prüfdienststelle für Handfeuerwaffen"), also conducts quality control tests. Arms and ammunition tested this way is now divided into three groups, but from 1950 until 1961, the proof house had four such classifications.

PROOF MARKS USED BY SUHL 1945–1950

First black powder proof, also known as material proof.

Final black powder proof.

Final proof with smokeless powder.

Mark of the Suhl proof house.

349 Date of proof, here March 1949.

PROOF MARKS USED BY SUHL AFTER 1950

First black powder proof for smoothbored barrels.

First black powder proof for rifled barrels.

Final proof.

Inspection mark.

Repair proof.

Choke-bored barrel mark.

Proof with nitro powder.

Suhl proof house mark.

660 — Date of proof, here June 1960.

Quality indicating mark, here indicating "Outstanding Quality."

Quality indicating mark, here indicating "Good Quality."

Quality indicating mark, here indicating "Utility Quality."

This mark, in use between 1950–1961, designated "Special Quality" guns which was yet another classification between "Outstanding" and "Good" quality.

THE GERMAN DEMOCRATIC REPUBLIC
or East Germany

On 14 June, 1974, new proof laws for East Germany went into effect. The new law affects all firearms and self-contained ammunition as called for by the proof law of 8 August, 1968, as well as all shooting devices, ammunition and shells as set forth in the proof law of 14 August, 1968.

This new law applies to the armed organizations of the German Democratic Republic (DDR) only when agreement has been reached between the Amt für Standardisierung, Meßwesen und Warenprüfung or ASMW (Office of Standards, Measures and Quality Control—OSMQC) and the appropriate Office of the Organization. The obligatory registration and proof remains in the hands of the states' quality control offices.

The OSMQC will establish a special department for firearms, and this will then act as the official proof authority.

Obligatory Proof

The following products must undergo proof:
All firearms, such as rifles, shotguns, combination guns used for hunting, smallbore rifles, Flobert rifles, all short rifles, semiautomatic pistols and revolvers, including flare and signal pistols.

Also subject to proof are all ballistic devices used to test the ballistic performance of ammunition, this to include all test barrels, test receivers, etc., used for measuring chamber pressure, bullet or shot velocities, shot patterns and the like.

Insert barrels and interchangeable barrels—that is barrels that can be exchanged without the use of tools—must also undergo proof, as must all ammunition of the self-contained type.

Shooting devices, such as stun guns, power-actuated tools, stud drivers, and all other such items operated by means of the discharge of a cartridge must undergo proof firing. Included also are those pieces of equipment which fire a solid projectile by means of air pressure, spring pressure, CO_2 cartridges or similar means of propelling a projectile.

Also included are gas, blank and starter pistols and revolvers, including all such devices which fire any type of chemical charge. Ammunition designed to be fired in these guns and devices must also be proofed.

Insert barrels and interchangeable barrels are to be tested with an extra heavy proof load. The use of insert barrels is permissible only in firearms which are fully functional and are designed for use with insert barrels.

The repair proof, required when a major part of the gun has either been repaired or replaced, was also maintained. This does not include already proofed barrels or barrels which can be interchanged whithout the use of tools or other mechanical devices.

Also open to examination and proof are the chambers of any gun or shooting device or machine that utilizes any liquid or gaseous propellant. Essential gun parts which can be finished with hand tools must be examined, as well as those parts which affect the performance and durability of a gun or firing device.

All guns, shooting devices and other tools mentioned above must be submitted for re-proof even though they bear appropriate marks.

Any user or owner of a firearm or shooting device that he feels is either worn or has become unsafe to fire in some manner, may submit that product for re-proof. Similarly, a firearms owner may submit a gun for re-proof after repairs if he feels that the repair in some way affected either the strength of the material or the safety of the firearm.

Repairs and alterations requiring re-proof include: Any change in the chamber or forcing cone, reboring, or re-rifling of a barrel; removal of rust on exterior surfaces as well as in the barrel, or chromeplating of the barrel; any repair or work on the barrel or action that involves brazing, silver soldering or welding of the action. Any proposed welding must first be approved by the OSMQC office. Any removal of pits or dents or any other damage on a barrel also subjects the gun to re-proof. In case an action, action housing or barrel is weakened by mounting a telescopic sight or a sight dovetail slot is cut, the gun must be submitted to re-proof. Similarly, a change in the bore, chamber, or the extractor or ejector in top-break guns, calls for re-proof if a weakening of the chamber wall occurred.

Lining of barrel or action is prohibited, excepting liners for .22 caliber rimfire gunes after application to the OSMQC.

Re-proof is not necessary if essential parts have been installed on a gun already carrying proof marks, or when only cosmetic repairs have been undertaken, such as re-bluing.

Should it be found or suspected that a gun or shooting device was not proofed or may be out of proof, or lacks the official proof marks, then the owner, his agent, or the gunsmith must submit the gun or device, without firing it, to the OSMQC for proof.

Exempt from proof are:

1) Imported firearms, barrels and shooting devices which are marked with proof marks of a proof house that has been recognized by the DDR.
2) Firearms chambered for "Zimmerstutzen" calibers. These guns are usually chambered for small rimfire cartridges, such as the 4 mm round.
3) Barrel inserts for Zimmerstutzen.
4) Blank and scare guns or devices with a very low performance, which are capable of firing only sound-making cork projectiles or a priming mix without a projectile.

Further exemptions from proof must be arranged with the Ministry of the Interior and the OSMQC.

SUBMISSION TO PROOF

Whoever manufactures firearms or shooting devices in the DDR or imports such devices is responsible for submission of these items to proof.

The owner of the firearm or shooting device who made application for any gunsmithing work, such as rechambering or repairs, is responsible for submitting the item for re-proof.

The person or persons responsible for submitting barrels, locks and other essential guns parts for proof on an individual piece-by-piece basis, must, upon request from the OSMQC supply, free of charge, all those parts and suitable firearms that are needed to perform the required proofing.

Furthermore, at the request of the OSMQC, adequate amounts of the needed ammunition, cartridge cases, powder, or projectiles must be furnished free of charge for the required proof firing.

THE PROOF OF FIREARMS AND SHOOTING DEVICES

The purpose of the proof law is to ascertain that all firearms and shooting devices made or sold in the DDR are fully functional, and that they do not present a hazard to the shooter, bystanders and surrounding real property when the product is being used in the manner it was designed for. Furthermore, proofing also affords a constant quality control for all firearms and shooting devices produced in the DDR.

Proofing consists of: The preliminary proof, proof firing with proof loads, and final inspection. The proof firing itself can either be done as standard proofing or as re-enforced proof.

The Preliminary Proof

Actual proof firing must be preceded by the preliminary proof of a firearm or shooting device. This preliminary proof is designed to ascertain if the item to be proofed is of sound construction, has no obvious defects or faults. Barrel as well as chamber dimensions are checked to make certain that they meet dimensional specifications. At the preliminary proof, the product is also checked for headspace, proper locking, and the presence of the required maker marks as prescribed by law.

The standard proof cartridges must easily enter the barrel or chamber, and the safety of the product while loading and firing the gun must be ascertained.

It is also to be determined that the firing pin moves easily, that the tip of the pin is not burred, that the firing pin hole is round and that the tip of the firing pin does not protrude from the breech block. Also to be checked are: The trigger pull, which may not be too light and must suit the purpose of the firearm; and the safety, which must work flawlessly. In case of revolvers, the chambers must be internally finished and polished, the cylinder must be properly finished and must index perfectly.

At the preliminary proof, firearms, shooting devices and barrels may be rejected if:

1) The required identification marks are missing.
2) Parts are rusted or inadequately finished and polished.

3) Defects in either material or finishing are found, such as: Cracks or splits in any material; faults which can be traced back to hammering, welding, drilling or any other mechanical work; inadequate finishing of interior parts which would make it difficult to inspect the item after proof firing; poor soldering jobs between barrels, barrel extensions, ventilated ribs and the like; chambers which do not meet the dimensional requirements for the specific cartridge or shell.
4) Functioning is incomplete, or the item does not function at all, either during cocking or locking of the action.

Proof Firing

Proofing is to be done on completely finished guns or shooting devices, etc., such as barrels. An item may be proofed in the white, providing the further work on the product will not weaken any parts of the gun.

The durability of firearms and barrels is to be tested with proof loads if the item is designed to be fired with self-contained cartridges or shells. It is permissible to use the proof loads if the temperature of the powder is between 59–86 degrees F.

Proof firing is to be done with two rounds in the case of shotguns, rifles which develop a chamber pressure of more than 28,447 psi, all self-loading guns, and all interchangeable barrels.

All those guns not mentioned in the above paragraph are to be tested with one proof load. In the case of multi-barrel guns, each barrel must be proofed with the number of shots prescribed as if the barrel were on a single-barrel gun.

To test the durability of firearms where the magazine is separated from the barrel, as in revolvers, one shot must be fired from each chamber of the cylinder.

Barrels, locks, actions and other essential parts of firearms, submitted separately for proof, are to be proofed with the same number of shots prescribed for an entire gun of this type.

Should a gun, shooting device or barrel fail proof, either by gas leakage, barrel cracking or splitting, it is permissible to assume that the proof cartridge was at fault. In such instances, the proof firing is to be repeated, but this time any number above and beyond the prescribed number may be fired, not only with proof loads, but also with standard loads.

Should a gun or shooting device fail proof again, the item is rejected from proof.

Proof Firing Guns With Smoothbored Barrels

Standard proof tests are to be conducted on all 12, 16 and 20 gauge shotguns which are designed for the standard, that is non-magnum, shells which have an average chamber pressure of not more than 9428 psi (650 bar).

For the standard proof test, at least two proof loads will be fired, and at least once the following conditions must prevail:

1) At pressure measuring point No. 1, a standard crusher gage, located between 0.669–1.378 inch from the breech face, with a surface of 0.0465 inch, and with a copper crusher measuring .118 inch in diameter and .193 inch in height, must record no less than 12,329 psi.
2) At pressure measuring point No. 2, which is 6.38 inches from the breech face, a standard crusher gage with a surface of 0.0465 inch and a copper crusher measuring .118 inch in diameter and .193 inch in height, must record a proof pressure of not less than 7252 psi.

Proof loads for shotguns, with a powder temperature of 68 degree F. ± 35.6 degree F. (20 degree C ± 2 degree C), must reach the following pressure levels as a mean for 10 shots.

Gauge	Length of shotshell case less than 2.992"	
	Measuring Point No. 1	Measuring Point No. 2
16 and larger	13,085 psi	7254 psi
20 and smaller	14,507 psi	7254 psi

	Length of shotshell case longer than 2.992"	
	Measuring Point No. 1	Measuring Point No. 2
16 and larger	14,507 psi	7254 psi
20 and smaller	15,930 psi	7254 psi

After a gun has passed proof, the owner, maker or the person legally entitled to the gun, may request a re-enforced proof. Re-enforced proof is mandatory if the gun is to be used with magnum shells, or with ammunition that produces a chamber pressure of 9428 psi (650 bar). For re-enforced proof, two proof loads are to be fired, and the standard copper pressure gage at measuring point No. 1 must record no less than 17,405 psi. A special proof mark is used to indicate re-enforced proof.

Proof Firing of Guns with Rifled Barrels

The proof load must develop a chamber pressure that is at least 30 per cent in excess of that of the standard factory round. Should the maximum pressure of the standard cartridge not be determined by international agreement, then the mean of the pressure determinations of ten standard rounds is to be used as basis for making up the required proof loads which must deliver a 30 per cent higher pressure level than the mean of the ten service rounds recorded.

In selfloading guns it is permissible to fire additional factory or standard rounds with the proof load to ascertain that the gun functions properly with standard cartridges.

Proof Firing of Other Products

The proof load must develop 30 per cent more pressure than the strongest standard factory load.

Should a shooting device be proofed by means of energy developed rather than by chamber pressure, the proof load must develop at least 10 per cent more energy than the most powerful standard cartridge with the haviest projectile.

Inspection After Proof

After proof firing, the firearm or shooting device undergoes a visual inspection. During this inspection, the proof master looks for stretching, swelling, cracks and tears in the barrel, chamber and the locking system.

In multi-barrel guns with soldered barrels, the soldered joints are inspected.

During this inspection, firearms, shooting devices and barrels are culled and rejected if, during the preceding tests, one of these faults has become apparent:

1) The cartridge or load could not be loaded easily;
2) The device failed to fire, which is to be considered a failure of the device;
3) The device fired without having the trigger pulled;
4) The fired shell or cartridge case is not ejected or extraced properly, and this mechanism has failed;

5) The barrel or barrels have developed bulges, tears, cracks or any other defect;
6) There was any stretching in the chamber in excess of 0.2 per cent of the standard chamber diameter;
7) There was any swelling in the feeding ramp, throat or choke;
8) There was any weakening, or actual or incipient separation of ribs, ventilated ribs, rails, action hooks, or actual barrels separation, either total or incipient;
9) The receiver either cracked or was deformed during proof firing;
10) There was a stretching in the receiver of more than 0.004 inch in top-break guns;
11) Essential parts of the action either broke or were deformed during proof firing;
12) Either the action dimensions exceed the norm or excessive head-space was found;
13) Any other fault was detected in the arm, including the trigger system, firing pin, etc.;
14) The firing pin either pierced the primer cup or made inadequate contact to detonate the primer or fire the cartridge;
15) The firing pin did not make contact with the primer cup in the center of the primer, or, in rimfire guns, the contact between firing pin and rim of cartridge was not adequate to fire the cartridge.

Results of Proof and Proof Marks

Firearms and shooting devices which pass the proof tests successfully are marked by the OSMQC with the official proof mark which is to be applied on a major part of the gun or shooting device. The proof marks and their meanings are explained in the following table.

On request, the OSMQC will issue a certificate of proof for each firearm or shooting device that has passed proof.

Firearms, shooting devices, and barrel which do not pass proof are returned without being marked with the proof stamp or mark. The OSMQC will furnish information as to the reason for the failure of the product.

Should an important part of the gun, device or barrel fail, and should this failure be such that repair is not deemed feasible and danger to shooter, user and bystander is thought to be such that repair or replacement is not in keeping with current safety standards, the OSMQC may either make the part useless by mechanical means or simply mark it as "unseless" with a stamp.

Should a once-proofed gun or shooting device fail during re-proof, the original proof mark is to be marked out with an "X" stamp, and thus becomes invalid.

Proof of Ammunition

The proofing of firearms and shooting devices is considered complete only when the ammunition for the product is also proofed and the quality control is supervised, especially when such ammunition is guaranteed. No single cartridge of such ammunition may produce a higher than prescribed pressure level.

For ammunition and semi-fixed artridges produced in the DDR, the established standards apply and each round must conform to the standards.

The maximum permissible chamber pressures for rifle cartridges are listed and each round must meet the specifications.

In the case of imported ammunition, the already established criteria apply. The standard chamber pressure data for hunting and sporting ammunition is applicable as listed in the current bulletin. To determine the standard pressure, the mean of ten pressure tests is to be used. The pressure requirement is considered to have been met if no cartridge develops more than 15 per cent more pressure than the standard, and if the mean of ten pressure tests is equal to or below the established standard chamber pressure for this cartridge.

A certificate of proof is to be issued to the maker or importer of such ammunition, providing the ammunition has met all of the proof requirements, and the ammunition maker has complied with the packaging rules. An importer of ammunition may not sell his products or pass it on in any fashion until samples of such ammunition have passed proof, and he has met all the legal requirements.

Continuing Quality Control

The manufacturer's quality control laboratory is responsible for spot checking production lots af ammunition and records of each test must be kept. Such tests must include pressure determination, as well as conformation of the finished cartridges to the dimensional standards, marks and headstamp, and packaging identification.

Should laboratory quality control tests reveal that, in some domestically produced ammunition, pressure levels exceed the permissible maximum pressure, then such ammunition may not be sold or shipped. If such ammunition meets the requirements of proof ammunition, it may be used as such, but must be marked in accordance with the rules concerning proof loads. Such ammunition must pass the tests designed for proof loads.

The quality control of the manufacturer is to be supervised by the OSMQC.

High Pressure Ammunition

Ammunition for which a higher than normal pressure is permitted must be loaded in specially marked cartridge cases. Each such case must be knurled or serrated at the head for easy identification. Should this not be possible because of technical difficulties, then the case must bear an easily legible legend that indicates that it is not suitable for standard use. For shotshells, the work "Magnum" is sufficient. Rimfire ammunition must be marked with a blue paint which must be applied either on the bullet, the cartridge case or the case head.

Packages of such ammunition must also be clearly marked:

> "Achtung! Erhöhter Gasdruck!
> In normalgeprüften Schusswaffen nicht verwenden!"
> [Attention! High pressure cartridges!
> Not to be used in guns which have undergone standard proof only!]

The smallest packaging unit in which proof loads are packed has to bear the clear legend:

> "Achtung! Beschussmunition!"
> [Attention! Proof loads!]

This proof law became effective on 1 Septembre, 1974 when it was signed that day in Berlin by the President of the ASMW.

East Germany's Proof Marks

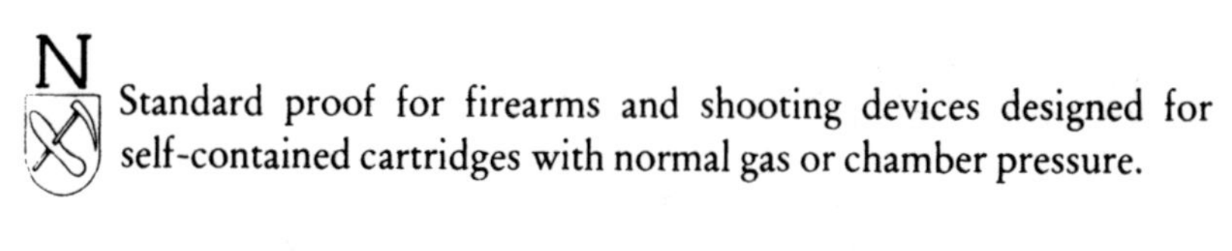
Standard proof for firearms and shooting devices designed for self-contained cartridges with normal gas or chamber pressure.

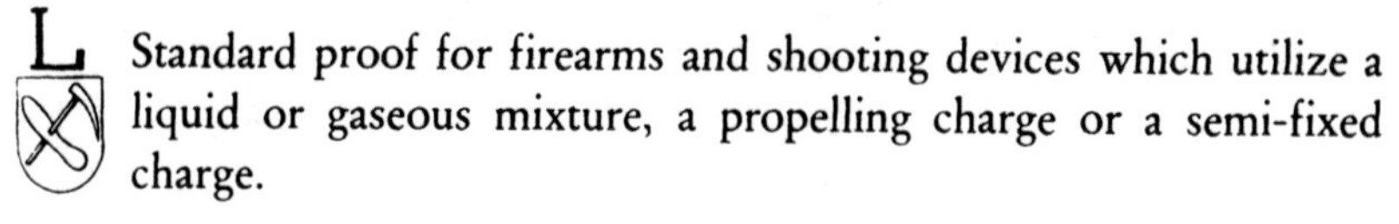
Standard proof for firearms and shooting devices which utilize a liquid or gaseous mixture, a propelling charge or a semi-fixed charge.

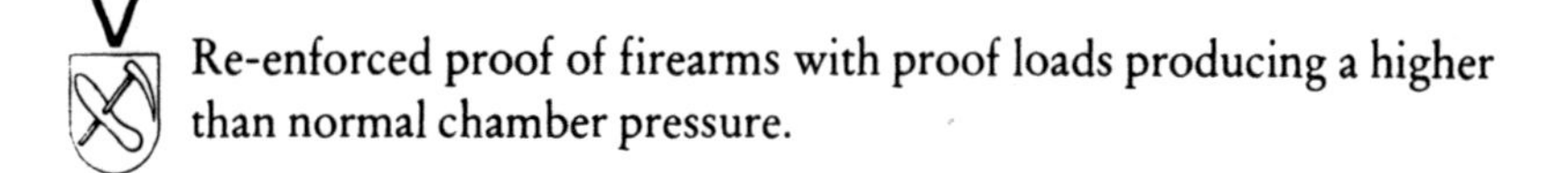
Re-enforced proof of firearms with proof loads producing a higher than normal chamber pressure.

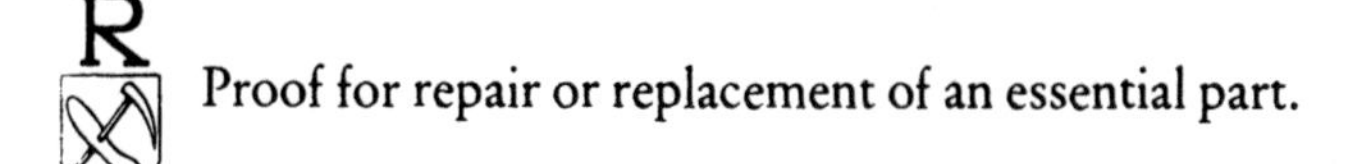
Proof for repair or replacement of an essential part.

474 Date of proof, giving month and year, here the date is April 1974.

ENGLAND

England is the classic example of a country with proof laws which have been in effect for many, many years. Because the English proof law is one of the oldest, it behooves us to devote some time to its study.

In the 15th and 16th centuries, England adhered to the long bow when other countries were already using some form of early firearm. Don't, for a minute, believe that the British did not realize the advantages of the firearm, but in the hands of an experienced bowman, the old English long bow was much more effective than the old matchlock. Then too, it was not until the end of the 16th century that workmen were successful in converting the relatively low-grade iron ore into a metal that was suitable for gun barrels. Although good gunsmiths worked already under Henry VIII, gunsmithing did not come into its own until the latter part of the 16th century.

At that time, the gunmaking art in England received a setback, and it was one that was to haunt the country for a long time. As a matter of fact, some of the repercussions of that period are still in evidence today.

The perennially broke James I made the gunmaking trade a royal monopoly and, as a consequence, in the year 1607 there were only five barrel makers in the city of London. He leased the gunmaking rights to the highest-paying nobleman attached to the Court. Obviously, the production of these gun makers was not enough to meet the domestic demand, and shortly after the monopoly was abolished, a thriving barrel import business started and anything that looked like a barrel found a ready buyer on the English market. This led to what we would now call a price war, and to a consequent lowering of barrel quality.

With an increase in wars, the demand for guns increased and it was not long before British gunsmiths were once again producing firearms. It was in 1631, not 1637 as often stated, that a royal edict was issued, permitting the formation of the first association or guild of gunsmiths and allied trades. The seven gunsmiths in this group were charged with the responsibility of keeping the arms of the citizen's militia in shootable condition. It was also stipulated that any arm made for this group was to be made by a gunsmith who had had at least a seven year training period. The Armourers' Company was granted the right of inspection and of all repairs, a step that more or less terminated the interminable squabbes between the various trades involved in gunmaking up to that time. The Armourers' Company was given the right to inspect the arms, and each such arm was then marked with the letter A below a crown. From then on, each gun sold had to be marked with the crown over A stamp.

On 14 March 1637, the gunsmiths banded together and founded the Worshipful Company of Gunmakers of the City of London. This name has been retained to this day, while the original name—"The Master, Wardens and Society of the Misterie of Gunmakers of the City of London"—is only known to gun historians.

The charter of the Worshipful Company of Gunmakers makes mention of private tests of proof, and this appears to trace back to barrel proofing which apparently stated in the early part of the 17th century. The original Worshipful Company consisted of 125 gun makers, of which 63 were citizens of London. The right to proof remained in the hands of the members, and this included the search for unproofed firearms which were then either proofed, or if the owner objected, the firearms were confiscated. This rule applied to the city of London and the surrounding country within 10 miles of the city line. It was forbidden to sell any gun in that area which did not bear the Crown over A mark of the "Gunmakers Company." The charter also specified the length of time a young man had to be an apprentice as well as the period or time he would be a journeyman. It was at this time that the Crown over GP was first used and to this day, this is the mark of the London proof house.

In the year 1670 the charter was confirmed and the power of the organization was extended. The Crown over GP was retained and yet another proof was added—the inspection after proof—and this was marked with Crown over V.

The two marks were always seen together, especially during the 18th century, with the name of the barrel maker often being sandwiched between the two marks.

In 1713 the "Gunmakers Company" built its own proof facility in Goodman's Field, Whitechapel, London, where it still stands.

One hundred years later, in 1813, the right and powers of the "Gun-Barrelmakers Company" was extended to cover all of England and Wales. At the same time, Parliament sanctioned the founding of a central proof house, this one being located in the hub of the British gunmaking industry—in Birmingham. For a while there was bad blood between the gun makers and the new proof house, as well as between the two proof houses.

The proof load for both proof houses was identical—the suitable round ball and four times the normal charge of powder. As proof mark, the sign used for many years by a leading gunmaker of Ketland was selected—crossed scepters. This mark had been used as private proof mark for some time, and now the letters BPC were added B P C to indicate proof, and the letter V was added to the old house mark V to serve as inspection mark. These mark remained in force until 1904.

In 1855 a new proof law was promulgated, and this has often been considered the basis of British proof law, although the proof law of 1868 has often been cited for that honor.

Essentially, the new proof law confirmed the role of the two proof houses and their backing organizations, as well as the respective proof marks. The new law also established five types of guns which had to undergo proof. This classification is of interest only from the historical point, since it shows the type of guns then prevalent.

Class 1— Smoothbored military arms.

Class 2— Double-barreled smoothbored military arms, all rifled guns with long barrels, both single and multi-barreled, the barrels made either from common or turned iron.

Class 3— Single-barrel hunting shotgun to be used with shot, as well as those shotguns commonly known as Danish, Dutch, Carolina or Spanish. These were flintlocks, named after the place of original manufacture.

Class 4— Double-barreled shotguns of all types for hunting to be used with shot.

Class 5— Revolvers and rifles using the rotating cylinder system, and breechloaders of all types.

This was also the first time that the temporary or provisional proof for unfinished barrels appeared in the law. A barrel that passed this stage of proof was marked [mark] from the London proof house, while the proof facilities at Birmingham used [mark].

In 1868 a new proof law was enacted, this one known as the "Gun Proof Act of 1868" Although little new was added, this law further strengthened the proof rules and their enforcement. Actually, this was the last of the British gun proof laws, and whatever additions have been made since then have been by means of ministerial additions to keep the law up to date.

At that time the British government was selling huge stockpiles of old military smoothbore flintlock and percussion rifles. All of these arms bore military acceptance stamps, both of the Army and the East Indies Company, but not the official British proof marks since, as military arms, they were exempt from the standard proof. However, if these guns were to be brought on the market and were in serviceable condition, many potential buyers believed that the arms would not require proof or re-proof. To resolve this dilemma and to indicate that arms were not only legally put into trade but were also serviceable, the ↓ Broad Arrow mark was introduced. Since many of these barrels were in questionable condition as well as being obsolete, two additional marks were introduced.

The capital letter **S** indicated that the barrel was serviceable, while the letter **O** meant that the barrel was out of proof and required re-proof. Either of these letters was applied above or directly on the Broad Arrow mark. If a barrel lacked either the "O" or the "S" stamp, it was to be considered as un-proofed, and therefore had to be proofed.

Penalties for avoiding proof are as severe today as they were then, and selling an un-proofed barrel called for a 20 pound fine. The same fine was levied against anyone selling a foreign barrel as a British barrel.

Imported barrels, and these came mainly from France and Belgium, were admitted without further proof, providing they bore the proof house marks of a proof facility that was acceptable to the British rules, as determinded by the London and Birmingham proof masters.

The first rules of proof for choke-bored barrels became effective in 1875. Instead of being proofed with round balls, soft No. 6 shot was being used, and the proof mark 12 B 14 M NOT FOR BALL indicated the gauge of the barrel at its widest point, excluding the chamber. The mark above indicates the London proof house, while the Birmingham facilities used 12 B 14 M NOT FOR BALL. Incidentally, the London proof house was operated by the Worshipful Company and is sometimes simply either called the Company or London proof or mark, while the Guardians of the Birmingham Proof House is sometimes called Guardian or Birmingham proof. Both proof houses also used the mark "B" for the breech diameter, and "M" for the muzzle diameter. On both choke-bored marks as shown above, the 12B indicates the gauge as measured at the breech just forward of the chamber, while the 14M refers to the bore diameter at the muzzle. Both of these marks have been discontinued. Choke-bored barrels were marked with the word CHOKE, and if that word was preceded by the letter R—R CHOKE— it indicated a rifled chöke.

Another set of proof rules became effective in 1887, and the most noteworthy feature is that the chamber length was now also marked on smoothbored breech-loading guns. The new mark indicated gauge at the chamber 12 C. If the chamber was longer than 3 inches, the letter "L" was added 12 LC.

Included in the new rules were also tables which indicated the bore diameter, in thousandths of an inch, for all gauges. The larger bores, that is from 4 bore to 10 gauge inclusive, were divided into three sub-gauges. The 8 bore, for instance, would then be marked 8, $\frac{8}{1}$ or $\frac{8}{2}$; the respective diameters were .835, .847, and .860 inch. The 11 to 17 gauges were divided into two groups, and thus the12 gauges were divided into two groups, and thus the 12 gauge would be marked either 12 or $\frac{12}{1}$ where the first mark would indicate .729, and the second one a bore diameter of .740 inch. Smaller gauges were given a single bore diameter designation. The gauge size was measured 9 inches from the breech end. These were the marks used by the two proof houses:

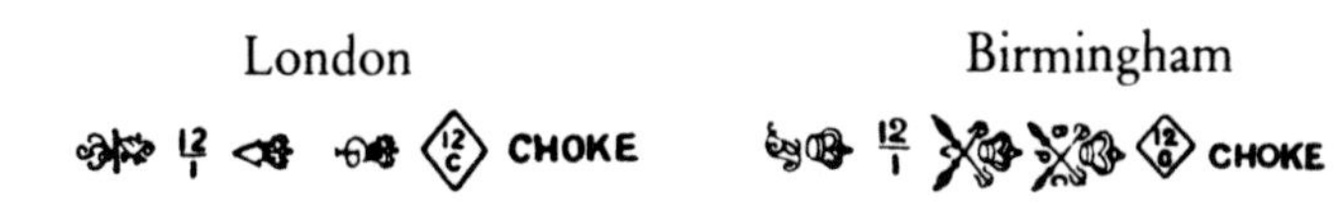

Express rifles were henceforth marked:

London Birmingham

577 EX. 577 EX.

The "NOT FOR BALL" mark disappeared at this time, hence it becomes an easy matter to arrive at an approximate date of manufacture for any gun marked this way—between 1875 and 1887.

On special application, a smoothbored gun could be proofed but once, but in accordance with the load set forth for final or definitive proof.

London Birmingham

Also new is the proof for nitro powder. To have a barrel or gun undergo this proof, it must have passed final black powder proof, and the gun was proofed with whatever powder the owner specified—"SCH" stood for Schultze powder, while "EC" referred to the powder made by the Explosives Company.

Both proof facilities had to determind the standard load of the respective powders and the load had to be calculated so that the proof pressure would be equal to the difference of the standard black powder load and the black powder proof load. This load and the powder were then marked on the barrel and became a part of the official group of proof marks. Should a new powder be developed, the proof load for it was to be determined the same way.

The proof rules of 1896 offered relatively few new proofs and were primarily concerned with nitro or semi-smokeless proof. It had been found that semi-smokeless powder in some rifles gave erratic pressures, and that henceforth, these rifles would be proofed with a special black powder.

	Proof Load		Standard Load			
			Schultze		Walsrode	
	Powder (grain)	Shot (grain)	Powder (grain)	Shot (grain)	Powder (grain)	Shot (grain)
12 gauge	114.2	726.8	41.7	493.8	30.9	493.8
16 gauge	88.7	581.8	37.0	435.2	—	—
20 gauge	95.7	509.3	33.2	378.1	—	—

These loads are based on standard loads developed by both proof houses. Should the proof applicant desire a stronger proof, he must request it in writing, and the proof load would be strengthened accordingly. Barrels proofed this way are marked

NITRO PROOF OZ MAXIMUM

The proof applicant may specify which semi-smokeless powder he wants used to proof a barrel only after a barrel has passed final or definitive black powder proof. The proof houses must then develop the suitable load, that is powder and shot charge, and this load may not develop less than 80 per cent and not more than 100 per cent pressure over the standard load. The standard load of powder in grains and shot in ounces with a suitably abbreviated powder identification is then marked on the barrel **MAXM (SCH. 45 Grs., SHOT 1,25 OZ).**

Rifled barrels of .303 bore diameter, the round being loaded with nitro and a jacketed bullet, as used by the British Army, have to be proofed with 46.3 grains of either Rifleite or a similar powder and a cylindical lead plug weighing 287 grains and being wrapped in greased paper. Rifled barrels for larger or smaller calibers than .303, which are to be used with nitro or semi-smokeless powder and a bullet that is at least 4 or more calibers in length, may be proofed at the request of the owner, the request being in writing. The proof must be conducted with Rifleite and a lead plug, the load being adjusted so that the excess pressure in the barrel is in the same ratio as the standard and the proof load in the caliber .303 barrels. On request, the proof houses would undertake to proof such barrels with a stiffer charge, but the barrel would only be marked for standard proof.

Proof Rules of 1904

These rules did away with a great many of the older proof rules, and added some new ones which were in keeping with technological developments. Dropped from the new proof rules were the regulations for proofing smoothbored flintlock guns, and also struck were the various semi-smokeless powder designations for smoothbore barrel proofs in their abbreviated forms, this being replaced with a list of powders suitable for proof. The former eight classes of firearms liable to proof were expanded to nine classes, and the two crossed scepter mark of the Guardians was replaced.

The final or definitive black powder proof executed at the Birmingham proof house henceforth carries **BP**, the BP indicating Birmingham Proof. The crown over BV **BV** indicates Birmingham Inspection. Semi-smokeless or nitro proof for rifled and smoothbore barrels, long and short, is now marked **NP** for the London facilities, and **NP** for the Guardians.

On rifled barrels the new rules called for marking the caliber in decimals of an inch, the weight of the standard powder charge and the weight of the heaviest bullet of the standard load **360 14 - 134**. This was to be affixed near the final or definitive proof mark. For Express rifles, the same load information was given, but an "EX was added **577 EX 167 - 610**

Barrels for semi-smokeless powder are marked similarly with the caliber, the "EX" if the barrel is an Express barrel, the final proof mark for nitro powder with the name of the powder used in proof firing, the standard load in grains, and again the weight of the heaviest bullet in the standard load **CORDITE 75 - 480 MAX**.

Barrels for cartridges similar to the military round are marked the same way, but **»NITRO PROVED«** is added.

One of the odder aspects of this set of proof rules is the "S&B" rule. Essentially, it calls for rifled barrels which are designed to be used with Shot ("S") and Bullet ("B") with the letters "S&B" near the mark for final proof. However, several British gun experts queried on this point admitted never having seen such a barrel.

If such a barrel also carried a choke bore, it was marked **R CHOKE** indicating a rifled choke.

Smoothbored barrels for semi-smokeless or nitro powder are marked with the shot charge in ounces as well as with **NITRO PROOF** with the actual stamp looking like this: **NITRO PROOF $1\frac{1}{8}$** If the barrel is destined to be used with shot and bullet, the Paradox barrels are an example, the barrel is marked **NITRO PROOF $1\frac{1}{8}$ SHOT.**

Rifled barrels are marked with the abbreviated name of the powder, the weight of the bullet, and to show that the maximum permissible load was used in proofing, the maximum mark, also in shortened form, is added **CORDITE 750 BULLET MAX.**

Smoothbored barrels which were proofed with smokeless powder and then in addition with semi-smokeless powder, were marked with the abbreviated name of the latter powder, the powder charge in grains and the shot charge in ounces **SCH 42 - $1\frac{1}{8}$** which translate into Schultze powder, 42 grains, and $1\frac{1}{8}$ ounces of shot.

Barrels for nitro powder, or nitro powder and black powder, were marked as having passed final or definitive proof with 

for the London proof house, and with NP when proofed in Birmingham.

Proof Rules of 1916

A new class or arms was added, the 10th, which included all military arms up to and including caliber .315. These guns were to be proofed once only for final proof, either with cordite or some other suitable nitro powder, and a bullet similar to the jacketed one as used in the service round. London used NP, while the other proof house used BM.

This included machine guns and similar weapons. It should be noted that Class 10 includes purely military arms, while those rifles using nitro powder service loads which are not military arms nor designed for military use, fall under the proof classification of repeating nitro rifles. As such, they were marked with the "NP" and a stamp NITRO PROVED on the barrel. In 1925, the caliber restriction was removed. Military arms were marked with the military stamp, while sporting rifles were given the "NP" or "NITRO PROVED" designation.

New in these rules was also the nitro proof for revolvers and self-loading pistols, the mark being "NP" surmounted by the crown if Birmingham proof, and the arm with scimitar mark when proofed in London.

To conserve critically short lead, commercially loaded shotshells produced during World War I contained a somewhat reduced shot charge. The 12 gauge loads, for instance, instead of being loaded with $1^1/_8$ ounces of shot contained $1^1/_{16}$ ounces, and since this load sufficed for British shooting conditions, the shot charge was not increased after WWI. At least, no mentioan of a load change was made in the proof rules of 1916.

The Proof Rules of 1925 Live On

Although there was a shift in the types of arms classified, the new rules retained the 10 classes. The extensive caliber tables underwent a number of changes. The reduced shot charge of World War I was increased and the 12 gauge shells officially contained 1 1/8 ounces of shot, although most of them were actually loaded with the reduced wartime load of $1^1/_{16}$ ounces.

In the 16 gauge $2^3/_4$ inch (70 mm) shells, the shot load was set at $1^1/_8$ ounces for the standard load, and the shorter 2 inch (50 mm) shell, was introduced under the Parvus name. The 3 inch (75 mm) shotshell was based on an American design, however the load given is only $^9/_{16}$ ounces of shot instead of the usual American load that contains $^3/_4$ ounces. One source also reports a "new" gauge, the .390 which carries 81 grains of shot in the standard loading—no other data about this one seems to be available.

The new Rules of Proof also specified that all foreign barrels proofed in England had to be marked: "Not English Make." The standard proof mark was used, but a heavy circle around the mark was added to make the foreign origin of the barrel immediately apparent. Considered as foreign, and unproofed, are all those barrels either totally lacking proof marks or those bearing proof marks which were not recognized under the British Rules of Proof.

Not accepted since 1946 are the German and Austrian barrels. Accepted are the Italian marks after 1950, as well as barrels made in Belgium, France and Spain.

Perhaps the most important point of the new rules is the compulsory semi-smokeless proof for all smoothbored barrels. In essence, this replaced the old final or definitive black powder proof.

The proof mark is the same as that used previously for final or definitive proof which is also identical to the mark used for voluntary nitro proof. Therefore, a currently produced British shotgun should have three proof marks in addition to the barrel mark and perhaps even a voluntary proof mark:

(1) Proof mark for final proof
(2) Inspection mark
(3) Semi-smokeless or nitro proof

The following proof marks are now valid:

London	Birmingham	
GP	BP	Preliminary black powder proof
GP	BP	Final black powder proof mark for use with nitro powder. The same mark is also used for the single, final proof with black powder for smoothbored muzzleloader barrels.
V	BV	Inspection or "View" mark which is applied after final proof.
NP	BM	Applied only to barrels of rifled military arms that have passed nitro proof.
NP	NP	Semi-smokeless proof of all guns.
SP	SP	Voluntary special proof performed with extra heavy load. This mark appears with the standard marks and the one indicating the standard load for this caliber.
R	R	Re-proof mark. Seen on black powder rifles which owner had proofed with nitro powders. Such guns also must carry the "NP" mark. Also seen on repaired guns which require re-proof.
12 C	2½"	New rule calls for marking of gauge as well as shell length for smoothbored barrels.

.360 3¼" or 9 mm 2.61" — For rifled barrels, bore diameter and case length must be marked.

NOT ENGLISH MAKE — All foreign barrels and complete guns, not bearing proof marks acceptable to the British proof houses, must undergo proof, are then marked with the standard proof marks in a heavy circle, and this mark. Letters are light on dark background.

Proof marks not shown here were obsoleted with this revision of the proof rules, but marks indicating loads, pressures, etc., remain unchanged.

In 1950, both proof house announced that henceforth all barrels which were chrome-plated or otherwise treated on the inside are to be considered unproofed barrels and therefore have to undergo proof. The Gun Barrel Proof Act of 1950 includes several other changes, and also does away with some rules which were contained in the Gun Barrel Proof Act of 1868 and which had been, in some instances, ignored for some time because they were sadly outdated.

To make "dating" a British proofed gun somewhat easier, the following list contains all the known dates as they apply to the period of validity of the proof marks.

British Proof Marks From 1868 To Date

London Birmingham

Temporary proof, in use since 1856.

Final black powder proof. The London mark was in use since 1672 in more or less the same form. The Birmingham mark was valid from 1813–1904. Since 1925, the London mark was also used to indicate semi-smokeless final proof for shotguns, but only in conjunction with the "NP" mark.

Inspection mark, London since 1672, Birmingham from 1812–1904.

Final black powder proof, Birmingham, 1904–1925. Then used with "NP" mark for rifles proofed with nitro or semi-smokeless powder.

Birmingham inspection mark since 1904.

In use from 1868–1925, this mark was used to indicate a single, final proof with loads designed for temporary or provisional proof.

Semi-smokeless proof for all guns, in use since 1904.

Mark indicating gauge. Prior to 1925, a three-inch chamber, but after that year, chamber length had to be indicated in inches.

Mark indicating gauge, in use since 1925. This shows that chamber is longer than 3 inches.

The proof mark used for chocke-bored barrels between the years 1875–1887.

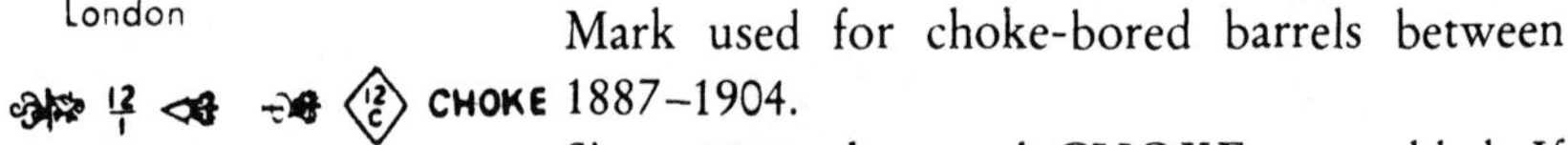

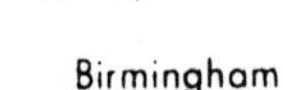

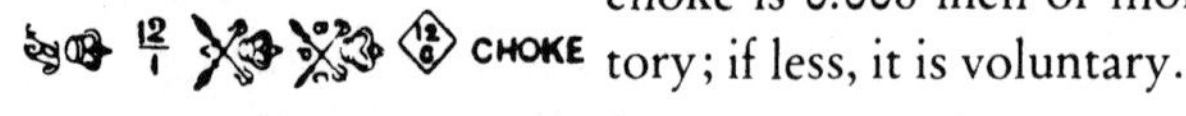

Mark used for choke-bored barrels between 1887–1904.
Since 1904, the word CHOKE was added. If choke is 0.008 inch or more, marking is obligatory; if less, it is voluntary.

London

577 EX.

Birmingham

577 EX

Designation for Express rifle barrels, in use from 1887–1904.

NITRO PROOF OZ MAXIMUM	Voluntary, re-enforced semi-smokeless proof, but actual proofing was done with black powder. In use 1896–1904.
MAXM (SCH. 45 Grs., SHOT 1,25 OZ)	Special, voluntary semi-smokeless proof after barrels passed the standard final proof. Proof load must develop no less than 80 per cent and not more than 100 per cent of the pressure generated by the standard or service load.
S & B	Mark for Shot & Ball found on rifled barrels.
R CHOKE	If barrels are rifled only near the muzzle, as in Paradox guns, this mark is affixed. In use since 1904.
NITRO PROVED	Breech-loading rifled barrels with bore diameter no larger than .315. In use between 1916–1925. After 1925, this mark was used for nitro proof of all barrels chambered for a military round, even if not of themselves of military origin or destined for military use.
London Birmingham 	On rifled barrels for military arms with a bore diameter not larger than .315. In use between 1916 and 1925. After 1925, used by both proof houses for marking all proofed military arms. Barrels were proofed with cordite, sometimes with a nitro powder, and were marked NITRO POVED or NITRO PROOF, depending on Class.
 	Voluntary special or re-enforced black powder proof. This mark was used in addition to the standard proof marks and stamp indicating the standard load.
NOT ENGLISH MAKE	Mark found on foreign guns proofed in England. Such guns also must have regular proof mark in circle.

360 14 - 134	Information marked on rifled barrels which underwent single, final black powder proof. First number indicates caliber (360), the second (14) the powder charge in grains, and bullet weight in grains (134). In use since 1904.
577 EX 167 - 610	Rifled barrels of Express rifles were marked this way between 1904 and 1925. As in preceding stamp, the numbers indicate caliber, charge and bullet weight.
CORDITE 75-480 MAX	Mark for smokeless powder proof for Express rifles which passed single, final or definitive proof. Name of powder or abbreviation, plus charge and bullet weight of maximum standard charge. In use 1904–1925.
CORDITE MK I 75 - 480 MAX	Replaced above mark after 1925.
4 dr 109 gr	On barrel which have passed special or re-enforced proof. Mark indicates the standard charge, and it should be noted that the powder charge may be listed either as drachmes or grains.
NITRO PROOF 1 1/8	Smoothbored barrels that underwent special or re-enforced proof were marked with the crown over SP mark and also this stamp which indicates shot charge in ounces. In use since 1904.
NITRO PROOF 1 1/8 SHOT	Use of this mark was restricted to barrels designed for shot and ball. Meaning of mark is identical to the one above. In use between 1904–1925.
CORDITE 32-750 MAX	Additional stamp found on nitro proofed rifled barrels. This indicates the maximum standard load which here is 32 gr. of cordite behind a 750 gr. bullet. In use between 1904–1925.

CORDITE 32-750 BULLET MAX For nitro proofed barrels designed for shot and ball. Note that word "Bullet" has been added to mark. In use since 1925.

CORDITE 750 BULLET MAX Same mark as above, except that charge weight is omitted. Used between 1904–1925.

SCH 42-1 1/8 On smoothbored barrels proofed with a semi-smokeless powder. Name of powder is abbreviated, powder charge is in grains, shot charge in ounces. Powder here is Schultze powder. In use since 1904.

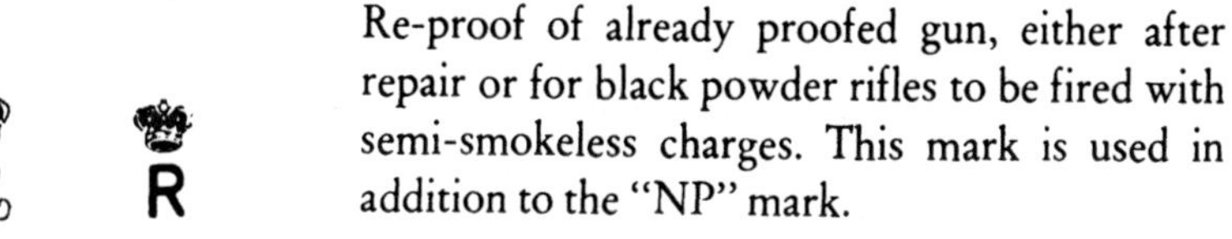

Re-proof of already proofed gun, either after repair or for black powder rifles to be fired with semi-smokeless charges. This mark is used in addition to the "NP" mark.

New British Rules of Proof are being developed, but as of the moment, no detailed information has become available.

SUMMARY

All guns proofed with smokeless powder must carry the "NP" mark on the barrel. Excluded are military arms which, instead of the customary "NP" stamp carry this mark 

According to German sources, British barrels proofed after 1925 with semi-smokeless powder can be fired with the standard semi-smokeless rounds made in Germany, providing the gun is in good condition and ammunition of the correst size is used. Such guns will be marked with the case length. Guns not marked this way, or perhaps with the LC mark, should be submitted to a gunsmith for examination or should be submitted to a German proof house for re-proof.

NEW BRITISH PROOF MARKS

Shortly after the new Rules of Proof were published in 1925, work was begun to update and modernize the entire proof system. It took almost 30 years before the new Rules of Proof were published in October 1954 and became effective on 1 February, 1955.

The following major changes were made in British proof laws. *Pressure:* The pressure of the proof loads has been fixed. As basis for this, the highest mean pressure of the standard load is used. For smooth-bored barrels, the proof load pressure is increased 60–80 per cent, while the proof pressure for rifled barrels is increased 30–45 per cent. The maximum of the mean pressure levels of the standard load is to be marked on the flats of the barrel, or directly on the barrel in tons-per-square-inch. [1 ton/in = 2240 psi = 157.49 kg/cm]

Ammunition makers now must list the highest mean pressure on the package. It was recognized that the actual proof firing and the subsequent inspection were one step in the proof procedure, and therefore the inspection mark V of the Gunmaker's Company and the BV of Birmingham were eliminated. Henceforth, London would use GP while Birmingham would use BP as final or definitive proof mark.

It was then assumed that few, if any, black powder hunting guns would be produced—the revival of black powder shooting had not yet reached England—and that henceforth those barrels designed for black powder use would be proofed with semi-smokeless powder. Barrels proofed in London now carry NP, while those proofed in Birmingham are marked with BNP, which is a combination of the "PB" and the "NP" marks. The "NITRO PROOF" and the "NITRO PROVED" stamps were eliminated.

Should a black powder proof be requested, a special mark is used. London now marks "NOT NITRO," while Birmingham marks such guns with "BLACK POWDER." This should do much to prevent any possible accidents where shooters use the wrong powder in a gun with a weaker proof.

Foreign barrels, which do not bear proof marks accepted by the British proof houses, are now proofed the same way British barrels are proofed. Since 1925 the standard proof mark with a heavy circle surrounding it denotes foreign made and this practice is being continued, but the stamp "NOT ENGLISCH MAKE" has been eliminated. Imported barrels must continue to be marked with the name and location of the maker, and in essence this only indicates that the Board of Trade rather than the proof houses made these import decisions.

The preliminary and voluntary proof for single-barrel shotgun barrels was also eliminated. It was felt that the second and obligatory proof was adequate to find any dangerous faults. This also served to reduce the workload at the Birmingham proof facility where almost 20,000 such barrels were proofed annually prior to this change in the rules.

The stamp "CHOKE" was obsolted and now barrels are marked with the bore diameter in decimals of an inch. This makes it possible to determine if any changes have been made in the barrel when the gun or barrel is submitted for re-proof. The gauge and case length designations remain identical. The special mark used to designate rifled barrels for military calibers was also discontinued.

The Rules of Proof for 1925 contained 10 classes of guns and barrels subject to proof. There were three classes concerned with muzzle-loading guns, and three for rifled barrels. The Rules of Proof for 1955 contained but four classes:

First Class: Breechloading shotguns with smoothbored barrels for standard gauges.

Second Class: Breechloading rifles chambered for standard calibers.

Third Class: Revolvers and semiautomatic pistols chambered for standard calibers.

Fourth Class: All other guns, including those especially designed for black powder use, harpoon guns, stun guns and cattle killers, power-actuated stud drivers and other such devices which must pass proof prior to being sold.

In keeping with other modern proof laws, the new British proof rules contain diemensional data for chambers, barrels, cartridge cases and shotshell cases.

As before, barrels designed for semi-smokeless powder loads are proofed with a special black powder designed for proof firing. The semi-smokeless British powders give too high a chamber pressure when used for such proofing. If and when more suitable powders are developed for proof, they may be used in both proof facilities without having to amend the Rules of Proof.

The number of proof marks in use were considerably curtailed by the new rules. For instance, the London proof house used nine marks for a 12 gauge, and now uses but six. In Birmingham, the number was reduced from 10 to five, and rifled barrels in caliber .318 now have six instead of nine possible marks.

Proof marks as seen on a .318 rimless nitro Express rifle

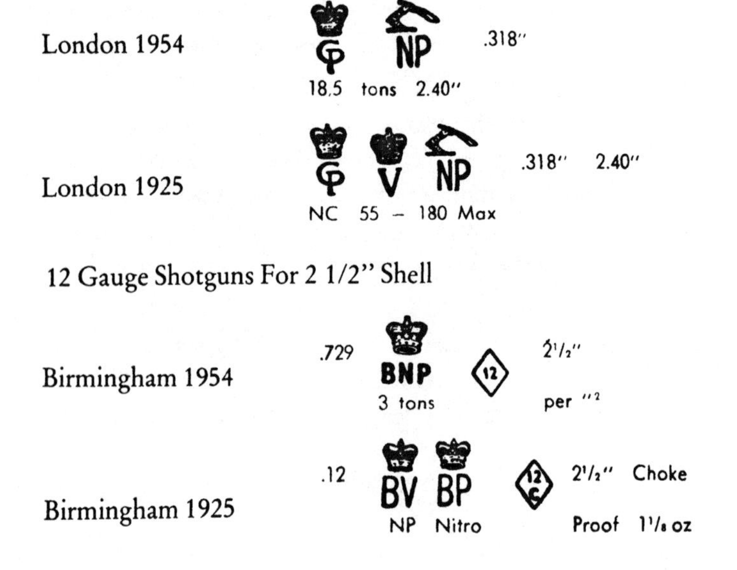

BELGIUM

The first of the Belgian proof edicts was issued by Maximilian Heinrich of Bavaria, Chief Bishop of Cologne and Bishop of Liege on the 10th of May 1672. The edict called for test firing of each gun made in Liege or of any gun imported into Liege. At the moment this became effective, it also became illegal to sell a firearm that was not marked as having been proofed in Liege. The proof firing was to be done in the city and each gun that passed proof was to be marked with the city's seal—a perron. The same seal is still in use today.

Maximilian's edict ran headlong into opposition with the guild of gunmakers. The craftsmen welcomed import restrictions, grumbled somewhat about the fact that guns in stock would have to be proofed, but they did not like the idea that their own handiwork, such as barrels would have to proofed. To make matters even worse, the proofing would be done in a public building and not in their own shop as they had done up to then. Their passive resistance resulted in simply ignoring the new rule. In August of that year a watered-down version of the ruling was issued, and in 1689 a totally new proof ruling was issued. This new rule was less stringent and gave the gunmaker's guild many of their wishes.

But the guild members continued their battles, and not until Napoleon issued the first proof law for all of France – which at that time included Belgium – did the proof law become somewhat more than a nuisance to be got rid of, or at least to be widely ignored. The Napoleonic proof rules of 1810 were strictly enforced – at least as long as Napoleon was in power. When the Dutch regime – Belgium was a part of Holland from 1815–1830 – tried to enforce proof, it had no more luck than Maximilian. A later Belgian edict fared no better.

The Napoleonic proof rule of 1810 introduced the first Belgian mark —the ELG in the oval. The proof law of 16 June 1853 finally settled the squabbles, and a temporary acceptance mark EL was introduced and the old city seal, the perron, also saw use again. The latter was used to mark barrels and locks for percussion shotguns after a final inspection. All barrels which passed proof were marked with the ELG in oval mark.

The proof law of 1853 produced the first really workable proof law and even today's Belgian proof rules are largely based on it.

All barrels delivered to the proof house were first inspected, the caliber or gauge was measured, and according to this, the proof loads were developed. After proof firing, the barrels were inspected once more, and the inspector affixed his mark to the barrel after he satisfied himself that the barrel was serviceable. The inspector mark consisted of a star above one or two capital letters *A *N *Æ After this, the temporary acceptance mark was placed on the barrel or gun. Once finished, the gun was re-inspected and then marked with the final proof mark, the ELG in the oval.

Accordingly, a properly marked flintlock shotgun would carry these marks:

a) A gauge designation
b) The final proof mark, ELG in oval

All percussion arms and breechloaders—note the very early mention of a breechloader which makes one wonder how many of them existed and how many may have survived over the years—would have both of the above marks, that is a) and b), plus

c) the perron or tower (literally "Steps," but "Tower" is the most often used translation)

All double-barrel shotguns must also carry the temporary or provisional proof mark which is the intertwined EL. All of these marks are still in use today and a complete tabulation of Belgian proof marks appears at the end of the chapter.

A Lefaucheux double-barreled shotgun would then carry these marks:

a) temporary proof mark for single barrels, the intertwined EL.
b) the final proof mark of the barrels, already regulated and soldered, the ELG in oval.
c) after fitting the barrels and fitting the action, then finishing the gun, the perron, or final proof mark is applied.

The proof law of 24 May, 1888, partly still in effect today, came next. Some parts of the 1888 law were later replaced by sections of the proof law of 10 August 1923. Between 1888 and 1923, some changes were made to keep the proof law abreast of technical developments, and these were introduced by means of amendments to the law.

To this date, Belgian proof laws provisions for muzzleloading rifles and pistols, and even the finest rifles are proofed with black powder. The smokeless proof is voluntary and can follow the obligatory black powder proof.

Muzzleloading guns proofed in the prescribed manner carry (E L G *), but it should be noted that there is no crown above this proof mark. If the gun has been also given the re-enforced or special proof test, the crown is added to the above mark. For instance, a Belgian breechloading rifle, found in Germany, on which the ELG mark appears without the crown, either on the barrel or on the action, can be dated to have been proofed prior to 11 July, 1893. From this date on, all Belgian barrels exported to Germany had to be marked with the crown over ELG mark if they were to be brought in without having to be re-proofed. On 18 October 1898, this rule was extended to cover all Belgian barrels, excepting muzzleloaders with standard proof.

The first or temporary proof of breechloading barrel is performed with a black powder load which develops a pressure of 11,378 psi at 8.6 inches from the action. At special request, a re-enforced proof will be performed, and depending on the proof load, this is then known as doulbe or treble proof. Here are data for three of the more frequently encountered gauges and barrel diameters.

Gauge	Bore diameter in.	Normal Powder gr.	Proof Shot oz.	Double Powder gr.	Proof Shot oz.	Treble Powder gr.	Proof Shot oz.	psi
12	.744-.709	231.5	2.05	231.5	2.72	277.8	3.17	11,379
16	.681-.642	200.6	1.69	200.6	1.90	239.2	2.61	12,801
20	.638-.602	169.8	1.48	169.8	1.98	200.6	2.29	14,223

Barrels which have undergone double or treble proof carry special proof marks. In studying the above table, it must become apparent that a double or even treble proof is not possible and that in effect, both of these proofs are merely special or re-enforced proofs. The Belgian experts feel that the standard proof load, even in the temporary or provisional form, will quickly show the suitability of the material used in the gun and that firing excessive proof loads can only damage the material or the gun without proving anything. Consequently, double and treble proofed barrels are rather scarce.

Those barrels which passed first or temporary proof, were then measured and the suitable gauge was then stamped on them. According to the proof rules of 1888, as well as those of 1923, the gauge indicated on the unfinished barrel could not be enlarged during polishing by more than 0.008 inch. Sould a bore enlargement become apparent during final proofing, the gun had to be re-proofed with a load suitable for the enlarged bore. After final proof, the gauge was marked on the barrel, and changing this marking resulted in a penalty. Should a marking be destroyed or damaged accidentally, the gun had to be submitted for re-proof.

A number of changes in the proof rules were introduced with the proof regulations of 1888. Some of these changes survived, others were abandoned. The various proof marks allow a fairly precise dating of a gun which, of course, is of interest to arms collectors, but of relatively little interest to hunters and shooters. The exceptions here are the black powder proofs which concern guns well over 50 years old and in which interest has been revived, thanks to the wide-spread popularity of black powder guns.

The first of the Belgian proof laws after the country attained independence, was the Royal Decree of 1 March, 1891. It was the earliest of the smokeless powder proofs on record. The powder to be used, then known as "wood powder" was variously classified as semi-smokeless and as smokeless, and was used for a voluntary proof of smoothbored guns with loads of shot. The proof master had the option of using either Schultze or EC (Explosive Co.) powders for proofing, and once a barrel had passed proof, this special mark E.C was applied. Later other special marks were introduced to indicate the specific powder used in a given proof. Among these powders were Cooppal, Müllerite, Clermonite, French T-powder, etc.

On 6 June 1892, another decree was issued, this one calling for additional markings of barrels which were submitted for voluntary proof and had passed it. Now the weight of the barrel in grams as well as chamber dimension in millimeters had to be added. Just how the marks were to be applied was not specified, but the proof house at Liege, for example, marked some barrels with $\frac{70}{20,6}$. Here the 70 indicates the chamber length in millimeters, and 20,6 (Europeans often use a comma instead of decimal point) is the diameter of the chamber just forward of the rim.

The decree of 11 July 1893 also specified that the bore diameter or gauge be henceforth determined 8.6 inches from the breech or receiver.

The decree of 30 January 1897 recognized the now widespread use of choke-bored barrels and the marking "CHOKE" for smoothbored barrels, while partially rifled choke-bored barrels were marked with "CH B RAYE." The bore diameter was marked this way $\frac{\text{CHOKE}}{16,3 \atop 17,0}$ The smaller number indicates the bore diameter at the muzzle, while the larger number gives the bore diameter 8.6 inches from the receiver. It was also ordered that the chamber be marked with the gauge, but again, no specific rules were established about the style of the marking. It was not until 4 October 1898 that the gauge marking took on a uniform appearance. The gauge was now marked ◇12 C◇ with the customary number designation and the "c" indicating "chambre." The enclosure of the two marks in the diamond strongly resembles the British mark.

The second and obligatory black powder proof developed a chamber pressure of 8818 psi with the following loads.

Shotgun Proof Loads for a Maximum Shell Length of 2¾ Inch (70 mm)

Gauge	Nominal Bore Diameter in.	Black Powder For Proof gr.	Soft Lead Shot No. 7 1/2 oz.
12	.729	179.0	1.67
16	.662	146.6	1.36
20	.615	138.9	1.18

With the new law, which became effective on 23 June, 1924, most of these barrel markings disappeared, and only CHOKE and CH B RAYE were retained. The bore diameter is determined at 8.6 inches (22 cm) from the breech and is marked accordingly, while the muzzle must have a constriction of no less than 0.008 inch, but without marking the degree of choke.

For example, the right barrel of a shotgun might be marked 18,4 CHOKE 18,2; while the left barrel is marked 18,3 CHOKE 18,2. This indicates that the constriction at the muzzle of both barrels is 0.0008 inch since the barrel is marked CHOKE. It also shows that the bore diameter of both barrels was 18,2 mm (.716") at 8.6 inches from the breech. The bore diameter of the right barrel after final or definitive proof measured 18,4 mm, while the left barrel measured 18.3 mm at the specified area in the barrel.

The new proof law also required the marking of the chamber with the gauge and the length of the shell (16-65). As can be seen, this Belgian mark differs from the British mark quite considerably.

The new proof rules also contained a provision that made it possible to proof shotgun barrels with black powder after the proof with a special smokeless proof powder load was completed. For this proof, the gun had to be completely finished mechanically, and all polishing and buffing had to be completed, but the gun was not yet blued. The proof load contained a special smokeless powder especially manufactured for this proof.

A 12 gauge 2 1/2 inch shotshell contains 1.27 ounces of No. 7 shot (British shot size), creating a mean chamber pressure af 12,090 – 12,801 psi for 20 shots. None of these 20 rounds may record less than 11,279 psi, or more than 13,876 psi. These pressures are to be taken at the first area in the barrel, and the second measuring location must still record between 2845 – 4267 psi. It should be pointed out here that in that second pressure area, the final black powder proof load pressure is 5831 psi—in other words, the black powder proof load produces higher pressures than the smokeless proof load.

The Belgian proof law also takes into consideration fast burning semi-smokeless powders, but what about the modern progressively burning powders?

The above-mentioned proof load data represent only the mean or average performance of the powder. The proof pressure for the 16 and larger gauge loads must develop no less than 12,801 psi, while the smaller gauges must create at least 14,223 psi. Guns chambered for longer shells must be capable of withstanding higher pressures, ranging between 14,223 – 15,646 psi, all measured at the first location in the barrel.

After a barrel has passed proof, it is marked with PV. The same mark is also applied to the chamber where the weight of the barrel is also marked.

For each gun proofed with semi-smokeless powder, the proof house is to issue a certificate of proof. This must contain: The type of gun proof and the degree to which the gun was finished when proofed; the serial number of the gun; the bore diameter in decimals of millimeter; the weight of the barrel or barrels in grams; total barrel length in millimeters; the length of the shell for which the gun is chambered; and finally, the proof pressure.

Aside from the smokeless powder proof, there is also another voluntary semi-smokeless proof where the proof applicant can specify which powder is to be used in this proof.

The following powders are suitable for proof:

Belgian: Clermonite, Müllerite and Cooppal, both in granular and leaf form.

French: J, S, M, R and T.

British: EC^{3}, Amberite and Ballistite.

Prior to WWII, the German Rottweiler leaf powder and Walsrode powder were used also, as were the Italian Acapnia, BPD and Sipe.

Only shotguns which pass the standard semi-smokeless proof are admitted to this voluntary proof. The proof load for these powder is determined by loading a shell with powder so that, after the addition of the shot charge, a standard roll crimp can still be made. This proof load must develop a chamber pressure that does not exceed that of the standard semi-smokeless proof load, that is between 12,801 – 14,223 psi. Guns proofed in this manner are marked with a special mark consisting of the Belgian lion and the abbreviated name of the powder, see below.

Smoothbored pistols designed to be fired with shotshells are to be proofed the same way a shotgun is proofed and are marked identically.

Rifled barrels for Flobert guns are to be proofed with one shot. The standard cartridge case is filled with a fine-grain black powder and the standard bullet is then seated in the case mouth. The following marks are applied to the barrel: The crown over ELG, the perron and inspector's marks, the crown over R stamp and the caliber designation in abbreviated form. Here it should be noted that the "22 C" refers to the

.22 Short and not to the .22 Central or centerfire, as is sometimes assumed. In this group of firearms, all of the rimfire guns, from .22 to 9 mm, are gathered together.

All of the long rifled barrels, regardless which gun they might be intended for, are proofed but once, either with black powder or with a smokeless proof load.

Full automatic arms and selfloading guns are proofed with semi-smokeless powder, and must be submitted in the white, but otherwise completely finished. This proof consists of three rounds, of which the first one must develop a pressure 30 per cent over that developed by the standard load. The other proof firings are done with standard factory loads to check the functioning of the gun and feeding of cartridges from the magazine. In case the selfloader is a .22 rimfire gun, the test with the two factory rounds are not performed.

If the proof firing is done with semi-smokeless powder, the special

W
PV mark is applied.

The double-barreled Express rifles are proofed with a semi-smokeless proof load and a certificate of proof is issued for each gun. This must contain: Condition of gun at time of proof (in the white, blued, etc); serial number of the gun; the standard name or designation of the cartridge for which the gun is chambered; if gun was proofed with lead or jacketed bullets; and the weight and length of the barrels.

At the manufacturer's request, the barrels for such guns can be given a temporary proof. For this, the barrels may be unrifled, but the bore diameter can only be .008 inch smaller than when finished. Barrels must be polished, but should be in the white. The rear of the barrel is to be closed with a plug, and the proof load is double the black powder load that can be placed into a standard cartridge case. The projectile is a lead cylinder 1½ times the wight of the standard bullet for the caliber. Barrels proofed in this manner are marked with

ℰ, plus the sign of the inspector. The finish proof is fired with a

proof load that develops a 30 per cent excess pressure over that developed by the standard round. In case of combination guns, that is rifle and shotgun barrels joined, then each barrel is to be proofed in accordance with the rules applicable to it.

Revolvers are proofed by firing one round from each chamber, the black powder proof loads developing a 30 per cent excess pressure above that created by the standard load for the particular caliber. For semi-smokeless proof, the proof pressure must exceed the standard pressure by 50 per cent.

Semiautomatic or selfloading pistols are to be proofed with three proof loads which develop a 50 per cent higher pressure than the standard round does. The caliber of the gun must be marked, either on the barrel or on the frame. Pistols with top-break actions, such as are chambered for the Flobert or revolver cartridges, stun guns, barrel inserts and other arms not mentioned previously are proofed in the same manner.

BELGIAN PROOF MARKS

This mark is used to indicate temporary or provisional proof. Found on barrels of breechloading shotguns, smoothbored muzzleloading and breechloading pistols chambered for shotshells, and centerfire rifles. This mark is also used to indicate preliminary acceptance on barrels for single and double-barrel muzzleloading shotguns.

Mark for voluntary, preliminary proof of unfinished barrels for muzzleloading and breechloading shotguns.

Proof mark indicating final proof of muzzleloading shotgun with standard load rather than proof load.

Three inspector's marks as they are found on barrels and actions. The names of the inspectors are kept secret.

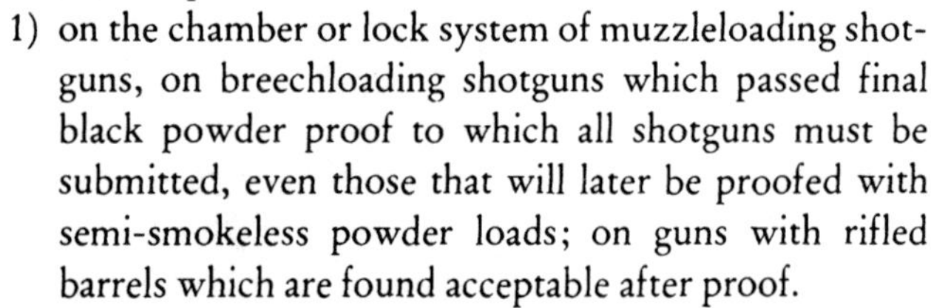

The famed perron mark. It is used:

1) on the chamber or lock system of muzzleloading shotguns, on breechloading shotguns which passed final black powder proof to which all shotguns must be submitted, even those that will later be proofed with semi-smokeless powder loads; on guns with rifled barrels which are found acceptable after proof.
2) on the barrel locking system or the chamber of Flobert rifles and pistols; on the lumps of breechloading shotguns after having passed final black powder proof, if the lumps are joined to the barrels.

The crown over oval containing ELG plus star is used to indicate:

1) barrels of muzzleloading shotguns that have passed a re-enforced black powder proof. This is a voluntary proof, and was introduced to keep abreast of the German proof law of 1891.

2) on barrels of breechloading shotguns that have passed final black powder proof.
3) on rifled barrels after a single proof.
4) on barrels of military arms, if accèptance of the guns was made dependent on proof by the acceptance commission; shoulder gun proof pressures have to exceed standard pressure by 30 per cent, that of handguns by 50 per cent.
5) on signal guns chambered for shotshells, and on the test barrels used for measuring chamber pressures.

The same mark, but somewhat smaller, is found:

1) on barrels of Flobert guns.
2) on barrels of selfloading pistols with an excess proof pressure of 50 per cent.
3) on barrels of top-break guns for Flobert or revolver cartridges with an excess proof pressure of 30 per cent when proofed with black powder and 50 per cent when proofed with semi-smokeless powder.
4) Also on cylinders of revolvers which were proofed with 30–50 per cent excess pressure proof loads.

Mark for voluntary double temporary or provisional proof on unfinished barrels.

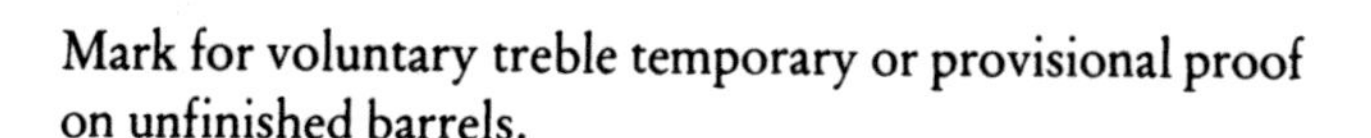

Mark for voluntary treble temporary or provisional proof on unfinished barrels.

This mark is found on barrels and locks of breechloading shotguns after voluntary semi-smokeless proof. Also on Flobert top-break pistols or on pistols chambered for revolver cartridges with semi-smokeless proof that produces a proof pressure 50 per cent over that of the standard cartridge. On barrels and on the most important action parts after single proof with three proof loads producing an excess pressure of 50 per cent. Also on barrels and cylinders of revolvers which have passed semi-smokeless proof, one shot with proof load from each chamber, producing the customary 50 per cent excess pressure.

On barrel and action of breechloading shotgun after gun has passed voluntary proof with a foreign semi-smokeless powder load that was found acceptable by the proof master. The mark consists of the Belgian lion and below the customary abbreviation of the powder's name.

This mark is applied to rifled barrels of:
a) Flobert rifles after proof with black powder.
b) revolvers after black powder proof and 30 per cent excess pressure.
c) Flobert top-break pistols after semi-smokeless proof.
d) revolvers after semi-smokeless proof and 50 per cent excess pressure.
e) muzzleloading handguns after black powder proof.
f) long guns.

This mark is found on barrels and the most important parts of the action of all firearms not made in Belgium and which do not carry proof marks recognized by the Belgian proof house; this stamp is applied after such a gun has passed Belgian proof firing.

This mark is applied to all Belgian guns not proofed in Belgium, but sent directly to a foreign proof house from the Liege proof facilities.

Proof mark applied to pressure barrels which meet international standards.

Gauge designation on breechloading shotguns, according to the proof law of 1888. Mark was retained in the 1923 rules.

On barrels and actions of rifled arms, as well as on smoothbored guns, the gauge size or nominal bore, plus the shell or cartridge case length as designated in the trade.

CHOKE 170	Latest means of designating the choke constriction, here 17.0 mm, in choke-bored barrels. This is the current mark used, prior ones are now obsolete.
CH.B. RAYE	Mark on partially rifled choke-bored barrel.
B. Plomb. or **B. P.**	This mark indicates that the rifled barrel was made for lead bullets.
B·Blindée or **B. B.**	This stamp indicates that the rifled barrel is suitable for use with jacketed bullets.

SUMMARY

On the whole, Belgian shotguns in good condition and bearing the mark of the Belgian lion above the letters PV, with or without proof powder indication and with a gauge designation such as this 

can safely be fired with semi-smokeless loads. Shotguns which have the gauge designation contained within a diamond, with or without indication as to what type of proof powder was used, should be examined by a competent gunsmith before being fired with smokeless powder shotshells and if there is any doubt, such a gun should be submitted for reproof.

All of these guns are at least 28 years old and may even date back as far as 1891. It should be kept in mind that during such a long period, metal fatigue can occur, even in the best-made guns.

FRANCE

As in other European countries, the question of who was to evaluate guns and how the job was to be done dates back to about 1700. According to some sources, the famed arms-producing town of St. Etienne began its own proof system during the early part of the 16th century, and 1700 is generally recognized as the official start of proof in France.

Already in 1729, there was temporary or provisional as well as a final proof system. These early proofs did not have separate marks, but there was an inspector's or proof master's mark, and the gun was also marked with the year in which the proof firing was performed.

On 17 January 1782 the first royal decrees regarding proof appeared, and these lasted, were added to, and changed every so often until the middle of the 19th century. The first royal order of proof did establish the first French proof mark – the seal of the city of St. Etienne. It was assumed, at that time, that stamping the proofed gun with the mark would weaken the entire gun. Thus, the crossed palm branches  were lightly engraved, but quite often, thorough cleaning of the gun also obliterated that sign.

During the French revolution, the trading and selling of guns by individuals was prohibited, but became legal again in 1797 when the old proof orders were once again put to use. In 1810, the Napoleonic proof laws became effective. Effective as of 14 December 1810, these new rules were a mixture of the old rules revived, plus some new concepts. For instance, the caliber scale was new; up to then, the gauge of a gun was determined by the number of round lead balls of bore diameter in the French pound, which was replaced by the metric system's kilogram. The old French gauge designations between 32 ga.-56 ga., instead of the 12–24 gauge system, were in use until 1868. Each French gun maker had to see to it that his gun underwent proof, and each factory was assigned its own proof mark.

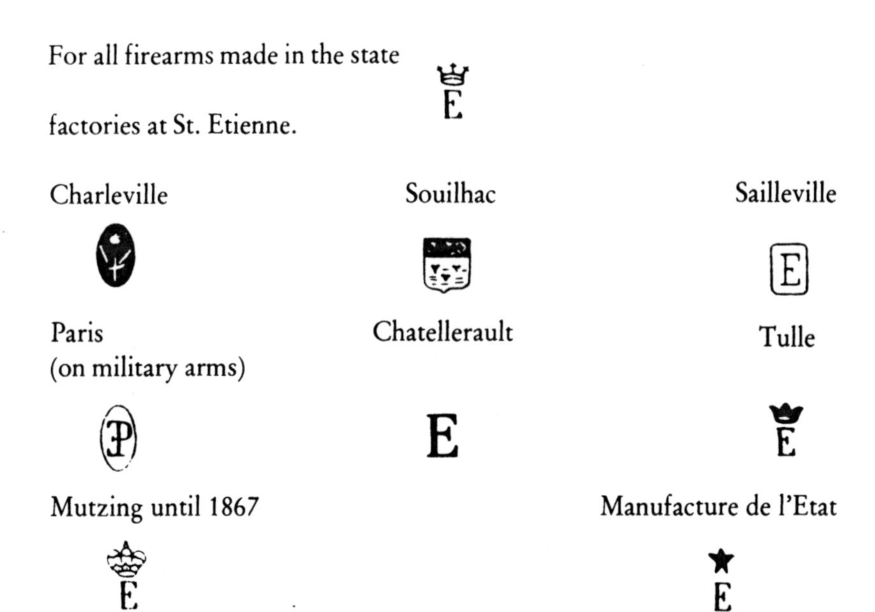

The old crown over E mark can still be found on the old French Gras rifles which surface once in a while. These were reamed out in France and converted to 28 gauge guns, and were then exported to Belgium where they were admitted without further proof. These guns carry the same proof mark twice, the first signifying that the gun passed proof after manufacture, the second one indicating that gun passed proof after the conversion to 28 gauge. Guns reamed out to larger gauges had to pass proof again in Liege before being sold in Belgium.

The proof load for a smoothbored 16 gauge gun, it was then known as 40 caliber, consisted of 246.9 grains of powder and a ball of bore diameter. A pair of pistols in the same gauge was proofed with one half the powder charge for each gun. Thus, each gun was fired with 123.45 grains of powder and a round ball of bore diameter. Re-enforced proof was indicated by marking the gun twice the same proof mark.

THE PROOF MARKS OF THE EUROPEAN STATES

After some rather heated arguments and disagreements, the mark for St. Etienne proof was agreed upon: SE . This became then the official mark for St. Etienne proof on 26 September 1811.

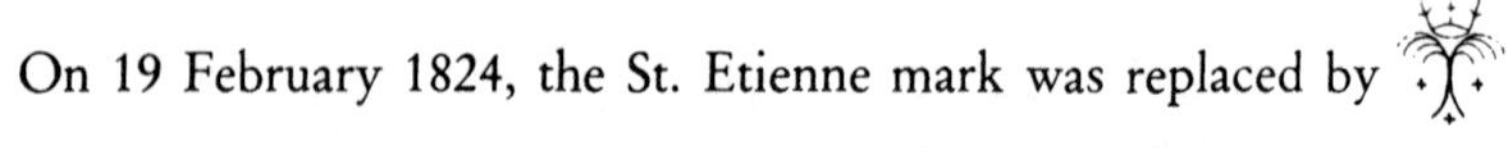

On 19 February 1824, the St. Etienne mark was replaced by 

According to official sources in St. Etienne, the old mark had undergone a number of changes as the government changed, and the official proof stamp somehow disappeared.

In 1856, the proof house in St. Etienne was taken over by the city's trade council, and again the St. Etienne proof mark was changed:

On 14 July 1860, a new law became effective, this permitting the private gun companies to alter the old military flintlock rifles to the percussion system. A new mark was designed, and this was to be added to the existing ones on the altered rifles.

The last of the French proof laws which made proof obligatory was published on 22 April, 1868. The proof itself and the rules governing the proofing of all guns was much stronger and more severe than any of the existing proof laws in Europe. Temporary or provisional as well as final proof for all rifled arms became mandatory, but smoothbored barrels were to be proof fired but once. In the short barreled handguns it happened frequestly that the large proof load of black powder simply would not fit into the barrel. Then the barrel was filled halfway with powder, then came a version of a modern shot wad, then a load of No. 9 shot was added until it filled the barrel – this was the proof load!

Since 1869, a new proof mark was used. At that time each proof house had but one stamp for all barrels proofed. Re-enforced proof, as already mentioned, was indicated by marking the barrel twice with the same stamp. Up to that time there was no preliminary or temporary proof, and hence there was no stamp for it. On 20 April 1879, the ministry of trade under which the proof houses functioned, initiated three new proof marks:

S^T ETIENNE for guns made in St. Etienne

for guns made abroad and imported into France

for guns made in France, but not in St. Etienne. This special mark was introduced at the request of the gunmakers of Paris. Many of them had their own proof marks, and Boutet of the Napoleonic era, as well as perhaps Bernard who made about 2000 barrels a year, were certainly major producers. Again, the double imprint of these marks signified re-enforced proof.

This proof law remained in effect until 1885. Once Parliament had approved the new law and the President had signed the bill making the law official, it was found that the terminology was such that, in effect, the new law cancelled obligatory proof in France. Proof became voluntary, and all in all, the French arms industry gained rather than lost ground and prestige. No French shooter or hunter wants to buy an unproofed gun, no foreigner wants anything to do with a gun that has not undergone proof – an example how the concept of proof can be perpetuated in the mind of the consumer without proof being compulsory. France joined the rest of the proof countries at the International Proof Conference in 1914, and the French proof mark is held equal to those of all other countries where proof is compulsory.

Despite the new law, the proof marks themselves remained unchanged for some time. In 1886 a new mark $\frac{\mathbf{E}}{\mathbf{F}}$ was introduced. The use of this mark indicated that the proof firing was done when the gun had been finished. On the 18th of October 1893, re-enforced proof of finished guns was recognized by this marking $\frac{\mathbf{E}^{S}}{\mathbf{F}}$, and this remained in use until 1897.

Unfinished barrels were admitted to proof in 1892 to make the French proof law more akin to the other European proof systems. This led to yet another mark

On 7 November 1895, the Parisian trade council was empowered to open yet another proof facility, this to be established in the city. The rules of proof, identical to those in effect for St. Etienne, were made public on 30 July 1897, but even before these became effective, semi-smokeless proofing went on in St. Etienne. The Paris proof house accepted the St. Etienne rules for semi-smokeless proof.

The load information marked on barrels and actions must be approached with some care since the burning properties of the proof powders and the composition of the powders underwent numerous changes. Thus, a gun proofed in 1900 was certainly safe to be fired with the load indicated, but with the changed powder composition of today's powder, it may become a potential bomb. Care is therefore indicated when shooting some of the older French guns.

As of 30 July 1897, the proof facilities at St. Etienne and Paris used the following marks:

Paris St. Etienne

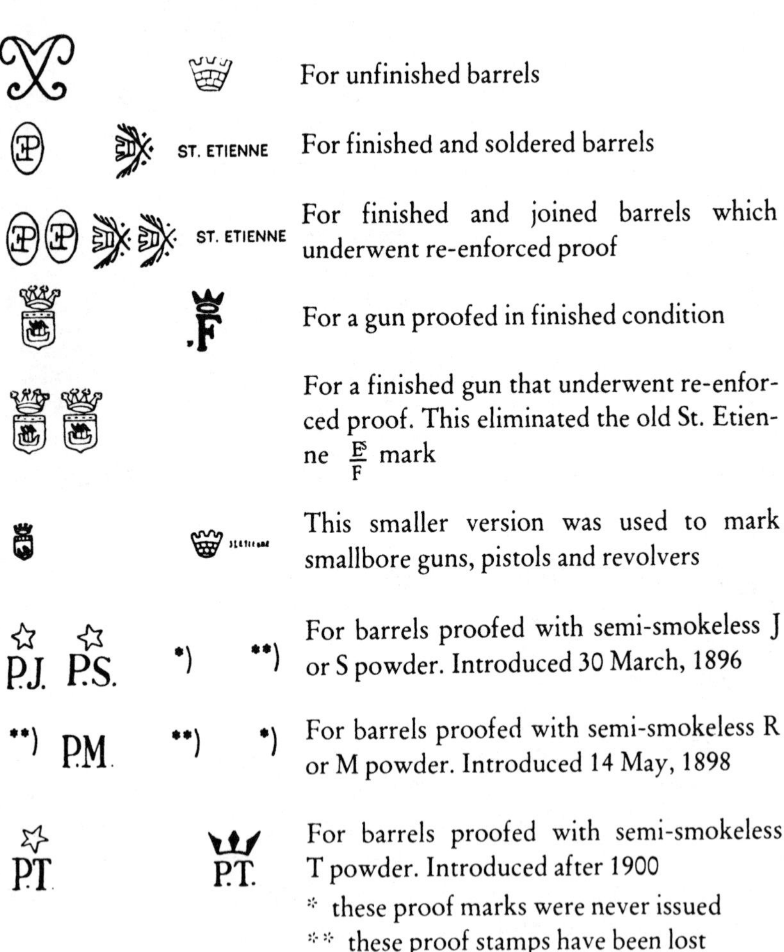

For unfinished barrels

For finished and soldered barrels

For finished and joined barrels which underwent re-enforced proof

For a gun proofed in finished condition

For a finished gun that underwent re-enforced proof. This eliminated the old St. Etienne $\frac{E^{S}}{F}$ mark

This smaller version was used to mark smallbore guns, pistols and revolvers

For barrels proofed with semi-smokeless J or S powder. Introduced 30 March, 1896

For barrels proofed with semi-smokeless R or M powder. Introduced 14 May, 1898

For barrels proofed with semi-smokeless T powder. Introduced after 1900

* these proof marks were never issued

** these proof stamps have been lost

Most of these marks are still in use, and it was not until 1901 that new marks were added. A more powerful proof was then being used in St. Etienne – still on a voluntary basis – and the Paris proof house was quick to adopt the St. Etienne proof system.

Paris   

Indicating double proof on finished barrel

St. Etienne I 

Indicating double proof on finished barrel

For the treble proof of a finished barrel, the Paris proof house used the same escutscheon mark, but four times as is used for double proof. For the same proof, St. Etienne uses

To indicate proof of finished but not joined barrels, the Paris proof facility used N.A. since 1901, while St. Etienne used N.A.

In 1928 this mark was eliminated, but was reinstated in 1946.

On the 18th December 1923, new proof rules were introduced. Retained was the standard and re-enforced proof which is not identical with either the double or the treble proof mentioned above, but the proof marks remained the same. Consequently, it has become almost impossible to attempt to "date" a gun by means of the proof marks unless the year of proof is known. While high or excessive pressures may well show up a fault, either in material or design of a gun, the exploitation of high pressures as a means of advertising became widespread in France.

The following table reflects some of the proof loads used by the Paris and the St. Etienne proof houses. It has been stated officially by French proof authorities, that the pressures recorded were determined by means of a system that differs from the usual one. It is true, of course, that all pressure determinations should only be used as a basis for comparison and should not be considered as absolute numbers. As can be seen, the listed pressures that barrels withstood during proof must be considered excessive when compared to the standard proof pressures used by most countries, and the use of some special pressure system is left open to question and discussion.

FRENCH PROOF LOADS 1901–1923

Re-enforced proof with strong black powder No. 2 and French soft lead shot No. 8

	16 Gauge			12 Gauge		
Proof	Powder gr.	Shot oz.	psi	Powder gr.	Shot oz.	psi
First proof, unfinished barrel	154.3	2.1	12,107	169.8	2.5	13,384
Proof of finished barrel	138.9	1.76	10,866	154.3	2.1	11,250
Re-enforced proof of finished barrel (épreuve supérieure)	200.6	2.1	14,934	223.8	2.6	16,114
Double proof of finished barrel	277.8	3.5	20,936	308.6	4.2	20,495
Treble proof of finished barrel	416.7	5.3	25,601	463.0	6.4	24,548
Standard French shotshell	69.4	1.0	6230	81.0	1.2	6472

France accepted all of the conditions of proof developed by the International Proof Conference in 1914, and the ministry of trade incorporated them into the French proof law on 4 June, 1926. As before, the proof powder was a special, extra strong black powder No. 2, and the shot was soft lead shot, French size No. 8, measuring 0.088 inch (2.25 mm) in diameter. Should a re-enforced proof be desired that goes beyond the proof load table, it can be developed and a proof certificate can be issued, however, no special proof mark for such a proof was provided for. The certificate must list the actual load used for proof, the barrel measurements and weight of barrel or barrels. Barrels submitted for such proof firing must be in the same condition as barrels submitted for standard proof.

The following French proof marks are in use:

Paris St. Etienne

Temporary or provisional proof of the externally unfinished, but internally fully polished barrels. Required pressure is 16,356 psi.

Standard proof for barrels designed for multi-barrel guns. Barrels must be joined, finished inside and out, except for last polishing. Required pressure is 14,223 psi.

Double proof. All barrels can undergo this proof, regardless of whether they failed or passed the preceeding proofs. Required pressure is 16,356 psi.

Treble proof, subject to the same conditions as double proof. Required pressure is 18,490 psi.

Proof of single barrel in finished state. Barrel may later be joined to another barrel. Proof is the same as that for finished and joined barrels.

The last proof and the proof mark were in use since 1901, but both proof and mark were discontinued in 1924. Thanks to the efforts of Manufacture National d'Armes de St. Etienne, who wanted to proof single barrels in the same manner as finished and joined double barrels, this proof was re-activated on 26 October 1946. It is now being placed on finished single barrels, wheter they are later joined or not. The same rule of proof applies to the Paris proof house, but it is not known if this mark sees much use in this installation.

If such barrels are submitted for proof in the joined condition, the same mark is used, except that the letters NA (non assemblé) are omitted.

All of the proofs mentioned up to now fall into the temporary or provisional class. For final proof, all arms are divided into three classes. Into the first classification fall long guns with smoothbore barrels, the second class consists of rifled barrel long guns, while the third class consists of handguns.
In use are the following marks:

Paris St. Etienne

Standard final proof with black powder. At the first location in the barrel, the pressure, taken with the international pressure system must be 8818 psi.

Re-enforced black powder proof. The pressure must be 11,379 psi at the first location in the barrel.

Standard smokeless proof with powder T. The pressure at the first location in the barrel must be 12,090 psi.

Re-enforced smokeless proof with T powder. If the S powder was used, the same mark was used, but the letter S was substituted for the letter T. Proof pressure was 15,646 psi.

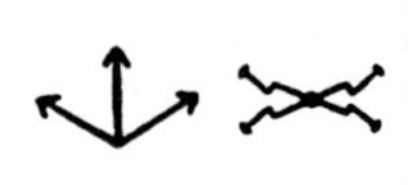

For the above proof, guns are submitted un-blued. In the case of a gun submitted ready for use, this mark is added to the proof mark.

All barrels submitted for proof must be marked with the stamp of the French barrel maker, but it is up to the person submitting the barrel for proof to specify what proof firing should be performed. Barrels lacking French barrel makers mark are considered as being made abroad. They are proofed in the same way domestic barrels are proofed, but after the proof, this mark AR.ETR ARME ETRANGERE is added, with the proof mark to denote the foreign origin of the barrel.

All guns that pass proof are also marked with the weight of the barrel, the length of the barrel in millimeters, the above-menthioned factory mark, the caliber or gauge and the length of the chamber. Only the proof house at St. Etienne uses the mark "Normal" and this is used if all of the above barrel and chamber information is within normal limits **NORMAL** as established by the Permanent International Commission on Firearms.

Marking the barrel length is interesting, especially since this is the first time that a major country clearly specifies this in the rules of proof. Perhaps it is because the French proof law does not specify choke-bore markings, although many guns from St. Etienne come with such a mark. It is assumed that a buyer of a used shotgun at some later time can readily determine if the barrel or barrels have been cut off sometime in the past.

Marking the chamber with the "Normal" stamp means that the chamber had to be measured at the proof house and was found to meet the standards established at the 1914 International Proof Conference in Brussels. However, the French recognize as "Normal" only those chambers which chamber the 65 mm (2.5 inch) shell.

Should it be found that the gauge or caliber marking of a gun at final proof is incorrect, and that the caliber or gauge is actually larger than indicated, then the caliber or gauge marking is to be deleted by having a line run through it in a horizontal manner. A new gauge or caliber marking is to be applied, just forward or toward the muzzle of the old and now invalidated stamp. Should the gun pass proof, it is considered as having been submitted in finished form. The St. Etienne "Normal" stamp may be applied if all of the measurements are found to be within normal tolerances.

Should a manufacturer desire that his barrels be proofed with either J or M powder, he need only request it. St. Etienne, under such conditions, will not issue a proof certificate, nor will the barrel be marked, but a "Bulletin de Tir" or Shooting Notice is issued. The Paris proof house marks the barrel with the initial of the powder used for proof. The reason for this rule is simple. It is not possible to get enough of either powder into a normally loaded shell to produce the pressure of 12,090 psi called for in the proof rules.

Cane guns which are still produced in France, as well as duck guns, are proofed the same way any other shotgun is proofed.

Proof of rifled barrels is accomplished by firing a proof load which produces an excess pressure of 30 per cent over the normal pressure. Repeating rifles are proofed with three shots, where only the first round is a proof load, the other rounds being standard factory cartridges. Flobert guns are proofed by filling the suitable cartridge case to the case mouth with an extra-fine black powder and using the standard bullet.

Rifles not chambered for a military round (cartouches de service) are given the same proof, whether single-shots or repeaters, as is prescribed for smoothbored guns. Rifles passing proof are marked with

A R   A.R. ST. ETIENNE The land diameter of the finished barrel may not exceed the one marked on the barrel during temporary or provisional proof. Should these measurements of the finished barrel be larger than marked, then the rifle must be re-proofed in accordance with the rules laid down for smooth barrels.

Handguns are proofed with special proof loads. Semiautomatic pistol proof loads must develop the usual 30 per cent excess pressure. Revolvers are proofed by loading the suitable cartridge case full of black powder and using the standard bullet. The load must be adjusted in such a way that the functioning of the revolver, that is cylinder rotation, is not impaired by too great an over-all length of the cartridge when the bullet is seated too far out of the case mouth. All handguns are proofed with as many rounds as the magazine or the cylinder can accommodate. One shot is fired from each chamber of a revolver cylinder, while the semiautomatic pistol is fired with one proof load, the rest of the rounds being standard factory loads. Handguns must be submitted either in the white or ready for sale.

Like other countries, France now proofs shotshelles in 10, 12, 14, 16, 20, 24 and 28 gauge for velocity and pressure, as well as proper construction.

SUMMARY

The French proof law does not recognize a general smokeless proof. Both proof houses use powder T, but sometimes the S powder is used, and in those instances, the actual powder charge for the T powder is given. At any rate, the first letter of whatever powder was used is marked on the barrel and/or on the action, the letter being preceded by the letter P. The Paris proof house uses a star above the letters, while the St. Etienne uses a crown, in addition to the other, already mentioned marks. German shotshells, providing they are of the correct length, can safely be used in shotguns proofed and marked this way. It should be kept in mind that most of the chambers of shotguns made in France are suitable only for the 65 mm shotshell – this in contrast to modern guns made in Belgium, Spain and Italy.

NEW PROOF RULES

On 12 January 1960 new proof laws were promulgated and these became effective in June of 1962. Obligatory or compulsory proof was re-established, and the new law can be broken down into four sections:

1. Proof of guns with smoothbored barrels
2. Proof of guns with rifled barrels
3. Voluntary temporary or provisional proof of smoothbored barrels
4. Re-proof and repair proof of all types of guns.

All guns submitted for proof must be finished, but may be in the white. Guns which have been completely finished are given a special mark (No. 1).

Prior to proofing, each gun is carefully inspected. Defective guns and those which obviously will not pass proof are rejected. Chambers and barrels are measured, and on shotguns, these data are marked on the barrel. On rifled guns only a caliber stamp is applied after the measuring. The internal measurements must conform to the norms established by the member countries of the Permanent International Commission on Firearms (Belgium, Chile, Germany, France, Italy, Austria, Spain and Czechoslovakia). For each proofed and marked gun a proof certificate is issued which also contains the pressure to which the gun was proofed and the pressure system used to proof the gun.

1. Prof of smoothbore guns (Shotguns)

Three types of proof were established for shotguns, and the choice of proof was left up to the proof house. However, only one proof was needed. There is a black powder proof, a standard smokeless proof, and a re-enforced smokeless proof. It should be noted that the smokeless proof is not compulsory. No matter what type of proof is decided upon, each barrel is tested with suitable proof loads, excepting in re-enforced proof, where the first shot is fired with a standard smokeless proof load and the second shot is then fired with a re-enforced smokeless proof load.

The proof load tables have been replaced with pressure tables and shotgun pressures now are:

Proof	Chamber Length (mm)	psi
	65	8818
Black powder proof	70	9245
	75	9672
	65	12,090
Standard smokeless proof	70	12,801
	75	13,512
	65	15,646
Re-enforced smokeless proof	70	17,068
	75	17,068

Guns which passed proof were marked on barrel and action with the appropriate marks (No. 's 2, 3, 4).

2. Proof of guns with rifled barrels, both long and short guns. Each barrel is to be proofed with two proof loads. The only exceptions are revolvers where a proof load is fired in each chamber of the cylinder. The proof loads must develop an excess pressure of 30 per cent over and above the maximum pressure produced by the standard load. Only smokeless proof is prescribed for rifled barrels. Guns which have passed proof are marked on the barrels and lock parts with the suitable stamps (No.'s 5, 6).

3. Voluntary provisional or temporary proof of finished shotgun barrels. This proof replaced the raw or unfinished barrel proof. The changes in the methods of barrel making made this change essential. Many guns are produced in France annually that are made in small shops and factories, and most of the custom guns come from such gun making establishments. These gun makers want to be certain that only the best material goes into their products, and hence they request voluntary proof of the finished barrels, either before or after they are joined. Only by submitting their barrels to proof this early in the stage of making a gun, can they be sure that the final product will pass proof once it is completed.

Barrels submitted for this proof must be finished to a certain degree. The as-yet-unchambered barrel must be polished inside and must be clean and free of any oil traces. After the preliminary or provisional proof, the bore may not be enlarged more than .008 inch or 0.2 mm. On demand, the proof houses will mark the bore diameter .004–.008 inch (0.1–0.2 mm) larger than actually measured.

This proof is usually fired with a fine-grained black powder, shot equal to No. 9 or 2 mm in diameter, and a paper wad. There is a choice of three types of proof: The single proof to 14,223 psi, the double proof with 16,356 psi, and the treble proof with a pressure of 17,779 psi. After passing proof, the barrel is marked (No.'s 7, 8, 9, 10, 11). If not yet joined, another sign (No.'s 12) is added.

If so desired, a proof with still greater pressure can be fired, but there is no special mark for this extra proof, and the extra high pressure proof becomes evident only on the proof certificate.

4. Re-proof and repair proof

All guns coming from countries not members of the International Commission must undergo proof. Great Britain, though not a member of the commission, has a special trade agreement with France that permits entry of British guns without re-proof. Also subject to re-proof or repair proof are all those guns which failed proof, or on which some work has been done that could have weakened either a part or the entire gun. Also subject to proof are guns which have had major parts replaced or repaired. If the bore of a shotgun has been enlarged as much as .008 inch, if the chamber has either stretched or has been lengthened by .197 inch (5 mm), or if the barrel weight has been reduced by more than 6 per cent, the gun must undergo re-proof. For this proof, the standard proof loads are used, and a special re-enforced smokeless proof is offered by the Paris proof house. Proof loads for unusual gauges are up to the proof master. In the Paris proof house, guns of foreign origin are marked with a special stamp (No.'s 13). Special proof marks were ordered for the re-proof and repair proof (No.'s 14, 15, 16). These marks retained the letter "R" for "réé-prouvée."

SUMMARY

Thanks to the new proof law of 1960, several of the old proofs have disappeared, and the entire system of proof is now greatly simplified. Furthermore, many of the barrel and chamber measurements were brought into line with those of other countries who are members of the International Commission. Aside from the five new marks for re-proof and repair proof, no new marks were added. When the new proof law became effective in 1962, the following proof marks were deleted: 17, 18, 19 and 20.

In 1965, the customary way of expressing pressure in the metric system, that is Kilogram per square centimeter or Kg/cm , was changed to the bar system, but since 1 bar is not quite equal to 1 Kg/cm but actually is 1.02 Kg/cm , the resulting proof pressures are somewhat higher than previously.

FRENCH PROOF MARKS

The parenthetical numbers in the preceding section correspond to the number preceding the proof explanation in the right column.

Saint Etienne	Paris	
		1. Sign added to final proof mark if gun was submitted in completed form.
F		2. Black powder proof.
PT	P.T	3. Standard smokeless proof.
PT	P.T	4. Re-enforced smokeless proof.
 ST. ETIENNE		5. Smokeless proof for short guns and smallbore guns.
 AR ST. ETIENNE	AR	6. Smokeless proof for rifles.
 ST. ETIENNE	EP	7. & 8. Voluntary provisional proof with a proof pressure of 14,223 psi.

St. Etienne Paris

9. & 10. Voluntary provisional proof with a proof pressure of 16,356 psi.

11. Voluntary provisional proof with a proof pressure of 17,779 psi.

N.A. N.A.

12. Additional mark for single barrels, used in conjunction with marks 7–11.

AR.ETR

13. Additional mark affixed to gun of foreign origin.

R

14. Re-proof or repair mark, proof with black powder.

☆ P.T. R

15. Re-proof or repair proof, proof with smokeless powder.

16. Re-enforced re-proof and repair proof with smokeless powder.

ITALY

Although one of the oldest of the gun-producing countries, with many ancient gun makers still active, the history of proof in Italy does not really start until the country joined the International Commission in 1920.

At first proof was on a voluntary basis, but this was changed by a royal edict on 30 December, 1923 – proof now was compulsory. This became effective on the 16th of October 1924 and basically the same rules of proof apply today. Of course, some marks were changed over the years. For instance, the royal crown was replaced by a five-pointed star.

When the compulsory proof became effective, two proof houses were established, one in Brescia, the other in Gardone Val Trompia. In 1930, the Brescia facility was temporarily moved to Gardone Val Trompia where the proof house and administrative office is now at the Beretta plant. The new proof marks introduced in 1951, however, were also planned for the Brescia proof house.

As must be expected, the Italian proof rules correspond with those of other countries which are members of the International Commission. A few exceptions were made to meet the demands and needs of the Italian gun makers.

The most frequent, though often voluntary, provisional or temporary proof is the one done on unfinished barrels. Although this proof serves mostly as a test of the quality of the material, it is now being conducted in conjunction with the final proof, with the barrel either still in the white or already chambered and finished.

The black powder proof has been on the books since 1931 and is now used exclusively for muzzleloaders. Breechloading shotguns are proofed with smokeless powder. Two shots are fired from each barrel, of which the first shot must produce a pressure of 12,801 psi for the 2¾ inch 16 gauge and larger barrels, while the smaller gauges require a proof pressure of 14,223 psi. For barrels chambered for longer shells, the proof pressure has to be increased proportionately. As a barrel passes proof, it is marked with the bore diameter in millimeters, the weight of both barrels in case of a double, the chamber dimensions, that is length and diameter, as well as the choke diameter, plus the proof mark. The chamber also is marked with the latter stamp.

It should be pointed out here that all guns proofed in Italy with smokeless powder must also carry the stamp „PSF“ in contrast to the black powder proofed guns are marked with „PN“ or *pulvere nero* – the „N“ is often mistaken to mean nitro, and if a nitro charge is loaded in a gun proofed for black powder, the results could be disastrous.

Arms with rifled barrels are proofed with a load that creates between 30–50 per cent excess pressure, the basis of comparison being the maximum pressure recorded by the strongest commercial load. Guns must be completely finished when submitted for proof.

Handguns are also proofed with excess pressures, and this pressure is recorded on the proof certificate that accompanies every gun into the trade.

The proof mark on a rifled gun with a long barrel is placed toward the rear of the barrel and underneath, where it is hidden by the stock. The proof mark is also applied to the action.

Semiautomatic pistols are proofed with one proof load, and with enough commercial ammunition to fill the magazine. Revolver proof consists of firing proof loads from each chamber of the cylinder. Proof marks are applied on barrel and frame in the case of pistols, and on barrel and cylinders in revolvers. The acceptance mark is impressed on the barrel.

Punt guns are included in the Italian proof rules. They are proofed with a black powder load that produces a 30 cent excess pressure, and guns, when presented for proof, must be completely finished and ready for the trade. Proof marks are affixed on barrel and action.

THE ITALIAN PROOF MARKS

Brescia   Gardone

1923–1950

Since 1950

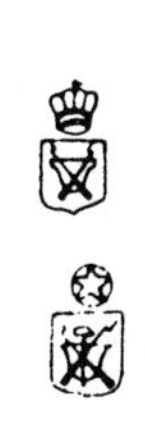

Acceptance mark of proof house, applied after gun has passed all proofs.

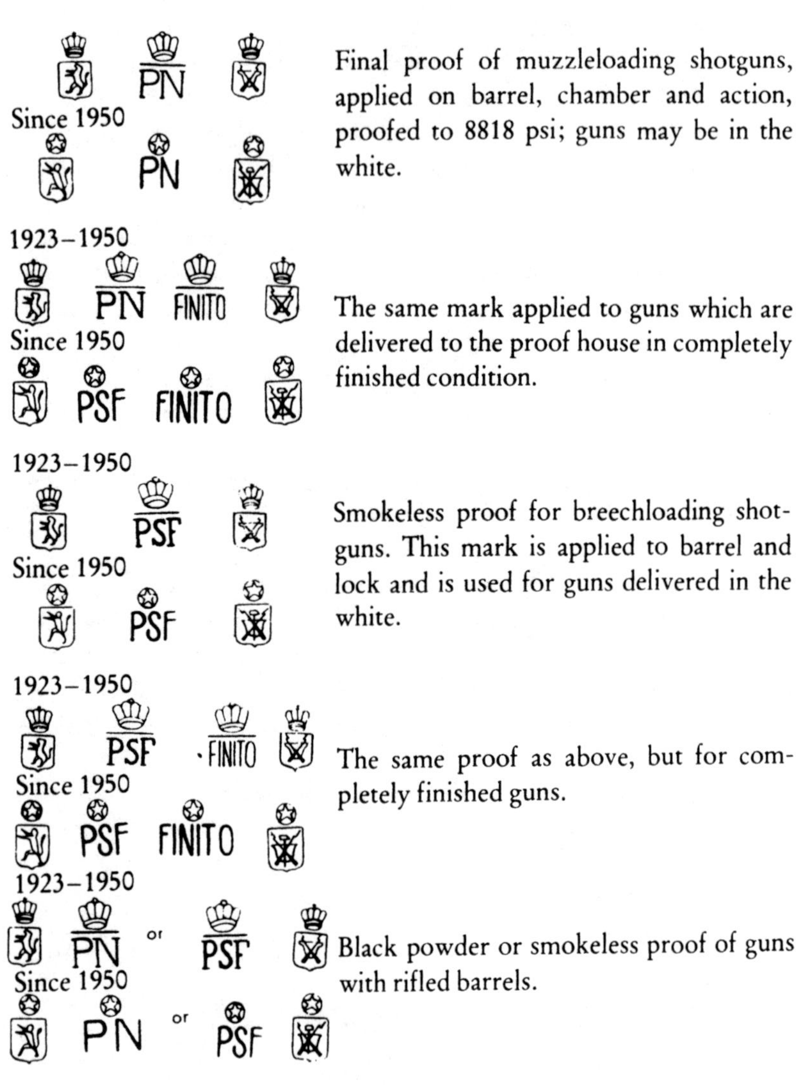

Final proof of muzzleloading shotguns, applied on barrel, chamber and action, proofed to 8818 psi; guns may be in the white.

The same mark applied to guns which are delivered to the proof house in completely finished condition.

Smokeless proof for breechloading shotguns. This mark is applied to barrel and lock and is used for guns delivered in the white.

The same proof as above, but for completely finished guns.

Black powder or smokeless proof of guns with rifled barrels.

Black powder or smokeless proof for smoothbored pistols chambered for shotshells. These guns are proofed with the same proof load and are marked as are breechloading shotguns.

1923–1950

Punt guns are proofed with black powder, with a load that produces a 30 per cent excess pressure. Proof marks are affixed to barrel and action.

Interchangeable barrels must undergo the same proof as the guns for which they are made or designed. They must be delivered to the proof house chambered, ready for use, and with a fitting stock.

The preliminary or provisional proof of unfinished barrels was recognized in the proof rules of 1923, but since then has completely disappeared. For the period from 1923 to 1950 was used to identify such single barrels. For the same period, the same crown as above, but in duplicate, was used to mark single or already joined barrels in the semi-finished condition. Since 1950, the crown has been replaced by two stars.

ADDENDUM

Some changes and additions to the proof law were made on 2 November 1962. New is the re-enforced proof for shotguns and the suitable proof mark. This proof is obligatory only for shotguns with chambers longer than 2 3/4 inch (70 mm), and guns with 70 mm chambers may be so proofed at the special request of the proof applicant. The proof pressure for this proof is 17,637 psi, and the proof mark is

PSF

Another new rule is that all automatic and semiautomatic guns are to be fired with as many standard rounds as the magazine is capable of accommodating. Up to now, this rule applied only to pistols.

The degree of choke on shotgun barrels, given in millimeters up to now, is henceforth to be marked with symbols.

☆	Full choke
☆☆	Improved-modified or 3/4 choke
☆☆☆	
☆☆☆☆	Improved-cylinder or 1/4 choke
CL	Cylinder choke (no constriction)

The five-pointed star is not encircled and is marked side-by-side.

Besides the proof mark, each gun that has passed proof, is also marked with the year of proof. This coded system began in 1945 with 1, and the roman numerals are continuous from year to year.

SPAIN

Spain has long been one of the major arms producing countries and guns carrying the Spanish proof mark have always been highly regarded – and rightly so. Just when the first proof firing was conducted in Spain is uncertain. Some historians believe that it was in the 16th century at the Royal Arsenal in Placencia, not far from the fabled city of Eibar.

The first of the proof houses appeared in Eibar, the center of Spanish gun crafts, in 1844. Actually, this was the year a royal order was passed on to Eibar, asking the city to build a structure for proofing barrels, the structure to be paid for by the city of Eibar. Prior to this and for years to come, proof in Spain was on a voluntary basis, and compulsory proof did not appear until 1923. This, like in Italy, was a direct result of joining the International Commission following the Brussels convention of 1914.

At the turn of the century, the Spanish arms industry's reputation was none too good, but in the years since, the skill and reputation of the Spanish gun companies and the many smaller gun craftsmen have taken over a leading role in Europe. The higher-priced shotguns from Spain, especially after World War II, gained a wonderful reputation as well-made and well-designed guns. Cheaper guns, especially revolvers and semiautomatic pistols, still suffer from the Spanish tendency to make do with cheaper raw materials which, in the long run, really are not cheaper but more costly. Use of inferior materials inside and in essential parts is all too common. Exterior finish is almost uniformly good, and Spain must be reckoned with as a major arms producer whose internal competition forces each gun maker to deliver a product that is just a little better than that of his competitor.

EIBAR PROOF MARKS PRIOR TO 1923

In use until 1910

1. Temporary or provisional proof of shotgun barrels with black powder.

2. Temporary proof of shotgun barrels with black powder and final proof of muzzleloading shotguns.

3. Breechloading under-lever shotguns. Final proof, gun must also have marks 1 and 2.

2ª P

4. Final proof of breechloading shotguns with action lever underneath the forend. Guns must also have marks 1 and 2.

5. Final black powder proof for breechloading shotguns with two or more locking lugs. Proof pressure is 10,667 psi. Gun must have been marked with stamps 1 and 2, possibly also with 3 or 4.

6. Final, smokeless powder proof for breechloading shotguns. Proof pressure is 12,089 psi. Before undergoing this proof, gun must have passed black powder proof, and should be marked with marks 1, 2, 3 and 5.

7. Re-enforced smokeless powder proof for breechloading shotguns at 12,801 psi. Gun must be marked with 1, 2, 3 and 5.

In 1910, marks number 1, 2 and 4 were replaced by:

8. Temporary or provisional black powder proof of shotgun barrels, replaces number 1.

9. Final black powder proof for muzzleloading shotguns, replaces number 2.

10. Final black powder proof for breechloading shotguns with action lever under forend, replaces number 4.

PROOF MARKS OF EIBAR PROOF HOUSE

18 July, 1923 – 14 December, 1929

11. Final and single black powder proof of double-barreled muzzleloading shotguns.

12. Final and single black powder proof of single-barrel, smoothbored breechloading guns. This mark should not be confused with numbers 22 or 23.

13. Final black powder proof for double-barrel breechloading rifles.

14. Final black powder proof for single-barrel breechloading rifles.

15. Re-enforced voluntary proof, requested by proof applicant, for single – and double-barrel shotguns. Now the pressure, in Kg/cm^2 is used as mark instead of the captial E.

16. Final proof of military-style rifles.

17. Single and final proof of non-selfloading pistols.

18. Single and final proof of selfloading pistols and revolvers.

Although no mention is made in the proof rules, it must be assumed that 15–17 are also suitable for guns proofed with semi-smokeless powder charges.

PROOF MARKS OF EIBAR PROOF HOUSE

14 December, 1929 – 9 July, 1931

The introduction of the following proof marks ended the use of the old marks 1–18. However, guns bearing the old marks may still be bought and sold.

19. Mark used by Eibar proof house.

20. Mark used by branch proof house in Barcelona. It is possible to confuse this mark with number 34.

21. Final black powder proof for single- and double-barrel muzzleloading shotguns. Minimum proof pressure is 8534 psi. Gun may be in the white but otherwise finished. Bore diameter is marked in decimals of millimeters.

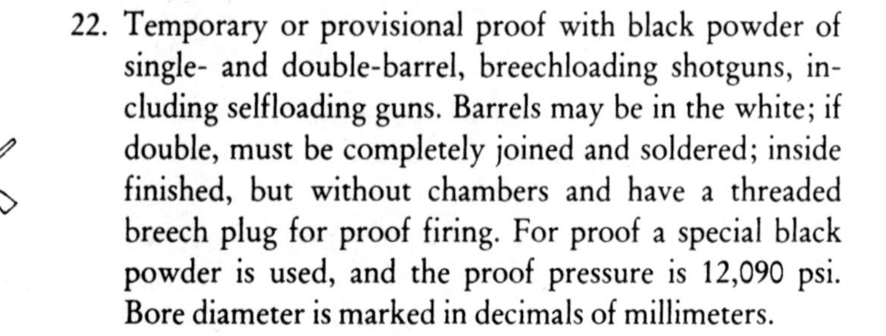

22. Temporary or provisional proof with black powder of single- and double-barrel, breechloading shotguns, including selfloading guns. Barrels may be in the white; if double, must be completely joined and soldered; inside finished, but without chambers and have a threaded breech plug for proof firing. For proof a special black powder is used, and the proof pressure is 12,090 psi. Bore diameter is marked in decimals of millimeters.

23. Final black powder proof, one shot per barrel, at 8818 psi, for single- and double-barrel breechloading shotguns, including selfloading guns. Guns must be completely finished for this proof and bore diameter may not vary more than .016 inch, in contrast to Belgian and Italian rules which have a maximum of .008 inch. If final caliber is larger, gun must be re-proofed and old proof becomes invalid. On barrel and chamber of proofed gun, the proof mark is applied, plus gauge in decimals of mm, length of chamber, and weight of barrel or barrels. Choke diameter is not marked. Selfloading guns are proofed with three rounds, of which the first one must develop 8818 psi if the gun is to be used with black powder loads, and the smokeless proof load must record 12,090 psi. The other two rounds are fired to determine proper functioning, and factory loads are used for this part of the proof firing.

24. Final proof of rifled long guns. Gun must be submitted in finished form. One shot from each barrel with a 30 per cent excess pressure load is fired. Basis is not the maximum pressure of a standard round, but the pressure generated by a standard, factory round. Selfloading rifles are proofed with four rounds, the last two rounds

being standard factory loads. If the selected powder does not generate an adequate pressure level, another powder must be substituted. The standard factory bullet is used for proof firing.

25. Final proof of long and short-barrel salon or Flobert guns.

26. Single and final black powder proof of pistols, selfloaders excluded, with rifled barrel. Two proof rounds are fired which must produce a 30 per cent excess pressure, the basis being the pressure of the standard factory round.

27. Final proof for revolver. One proof load each is fired from each chamber in cylinder. Proof pressure must exceed standard pressure by 30 per cent.

28. Proof for semiautomatic pistols. Two proof loads and two standard factory rounds are fired. The proof pressure must exced the standard pressure by at least 30 per cent.

FE

29. A special manufacturer's mark which certifies that bore and chamber dimensions meet the established norm as set forth in proof rules. Guns made for foreign sales, and chambered for cartridges that are not standard in Spain, lack this mark. In such cases, maker must furnish proof loads. Can be applied to rifled barrel and smoothbored guns.

30. Smokeless proof of shotgun barrels, proof pressure is 12,090 psi.

31. Re-enforced smokeless proof for shotgun barrels with a proof pressure of 12,801 psi.

Proofs 30 and 31 are voluntary and special application must be made to the proof master. Gun must have passed proof 23 before either of these voluntary proofs will be fired. Should the gun fail either of the voluntary proofs, all earlier proofs are cancelled, and gun is either returned unproofed or made useless.

32. Guns imported from a foreign country must carry proof marks accepted by the Spanish proof house. Should there be no acceptable proof marks an the gun, it must pass preliminary or provisional proof, then the suitable final proof. This mark is then applied to barrel and important parts of the action.

EIBAR PROOF MARKS SINCE 9 JULY, 1931

33. This Eibar proof house mark replaced mark number 19.

34. This Barcelona mark replaced number 20 between 1931 and 1935, at which time this proof house was closed.

35. Final proof for rifled pistols, excepting selfloading guns. Replaced mark 26.

36. Replaced mark 29 for guns made within specified dimensional tolerances.

37. Optional smokeless powder proof of shotgun barrels with a proof pressure of 12,090 psi. This mark replaced stamp 30.

On special request, the Eibar proof house will conduct pressure and velocity tests, as well as functional proofs on shotshells.

DENMARK

Relatively little is known about proof in Denmark, but there is little question that some sort of proof was known and practiced in the 16th century. Stockel, in his monumental work, indicates that Denmark had an acceptance stamp during King Frederick IV's reign (1699–1730). Such acceptance marks have been found on barrels made in other European countries. It can be assumed that such official acceptance marks are based on at least an inspection if not actual proof firing of the barrel, but since Denmark never entered the firearms export market to any degree and did not join the International Commission previously mentioned, little is known about the history of proof, proof methods or proof rules as they existed in this country.

DANISH PROOF MARKS

Proof mark on a 12 gauge autoloading shotgun Sjogren design, made by the Royal Danish arsenal, Vaabenarsenalet around 1906.

Barrel proof mark in effect until 1933.

Barrel proof mark in use after 1933.

Function and proof mark, presumably final proof.

Manufacturer's mark, this one indicating that gun bearing this mark was made by the Royal Danish arsenal, Haerens Vaabenarsenalet.

Two other manufacturing marks used by the

Hearens Vaabenarsenalet.

RUSSIA

The Russian arms industry dates back to the 17th century, and most of the early output was of a military nature. Although the guns were proofed, there was no proof law or proof mark.

The arms factory at Tula–sortimes also spelled Tule–made guns for private use and affixed a proof mark to those guns. Prior to World War I, there were plans afoot to initiate proof laws and proof houses – probably thanks to the International Conference in Brussels – but the war, and the revolution after the war, ended this project before anything could be done about it.

In 1920, the arms plants at Tula and Izhevsk were taken over by the State so that arms production for non-military guns was strictly controlled. A proof law for black powder and nitro powder became effective and proof marks were used. The marks were not standardized and changed quite frequently, but on the whole, proof firing was accomplished in this order: A preliminary proof with black powder, a final proof with black powder, and a final proof with nitro powder.

At the present, proof in Tula and Izhevsk is standarized, and the proof marks for both proof houses are distinctly different.

Proof for shotguns is as follows: Barrels for double-barrel guns are proofed with nitro or smokeless powder before being joined. The following load data for proof loads are used:

Gauge	Pressure-psi	Shot Charge-oz.
12	13,667	1.25
16	14,402	1.05
20	15,210	0.88

It should be noted that Russian proof pressures are given in the metric atmospheres rather than the customary Kg/cm^2 or the bar system.

Single-barrel shotguns are not required to undergo a preliminary or provisional proof. Instead, a final smokeless powder proof with the following loads and pressures is used.

Gauge	Pressure-psi	Shot Charge-oz.
12	12,198	1.25
16	12,932	1.05
20	13,667	0.88
28	14,402	0.71
32	15,207	0.53

The amount of choke is either indicated by means of bore and choke diameter such as $\frac{18.2}{17.2}$, or by means of numbers.

	Choke-in.	
No. 1	.010	improved-cylinder
No. 2	.020	modified
No. 3	.030	improved-modified
No. 4	.039	full
No. 5	.049	extra full

A rather unusual feature of the Russian proof is that each gun is patterned and point of impact is checked. Patterning is done at 38 yards on a patterning paper about 30 inches wide and high. This serves to verify the degree of choke marked on the barrel and also check functioning as well as point of impact. Gun factories have established their own quality control departments where functioning is checked before the gun leaves the factory.

Once in a while, a mark will be found on a Russian gun that indicates the type of steel used.

TULA PROOF MARKS PRIOR TO 1917

TULA AND IZHEVSK PROOF MARKS AFTER 1950

Temporary or provisional black powder proof.

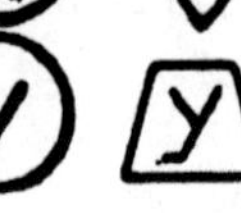

Final black powder proof.

УК Mark indicates not only final proof, but also patterning and point of aim testing.

NITRO НИТРО (Н)

Б $\frac{И}{Д}$ П ИСПЫТАНЫ БЕЗД. ПОРОХ.
3,5г

Final smokeless powder proof.

(К) Mark indicates the gun has been checked for patterning and point of impact.

НЕ БОЛЕЕ 700 — Mark indicates highest permissibles gas pressure with standard round.

До 700 ат АТМ. 700 АТМ.

(12) 16k K16x70 12x70

70mm $\frac{70}{20,7}$ $\frac{12X70,1}{20,65}$

Gauge, chamber dimensions and case or shell length.

BARREL DIMENSIONS AND CHOKE MARKINGS

$\frac{16,9}{16,2}$ Improved-modified choke.

ЦИЛ Cylinder choke – no constriction.

ЧОК Full choke.

◇ 12 C Full choke.

П-ЧОК Modified choke.

Modified choke.

Full choke.

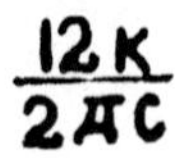

Full choke.

TULA PROOF HOUSE MARKS

IZHEVSK PROOF HOUSE MARKS

QUALITY CONTROL MARKS

MARKS INDICATING QUALITY OF STEEL

50РА 30ХН2 МФА 50-А 3ВХСА

This mark on a shotgun indicates that only paper shotshells are to be used in the gun. БУМ

These are the proof marks you can expect to find on a Russian double barrel shotgun made at the Izhevsk plant.

1. Provisional black powder proof.
2. Pressure generated by standard shell.
3. Final smokeless powder proof.
4. Barrel and choke measurements.
5. Year gun was made.
6. Serial number preceded by a letter.
7. Same as 4.
8. Mark of factory.
9. Gauge

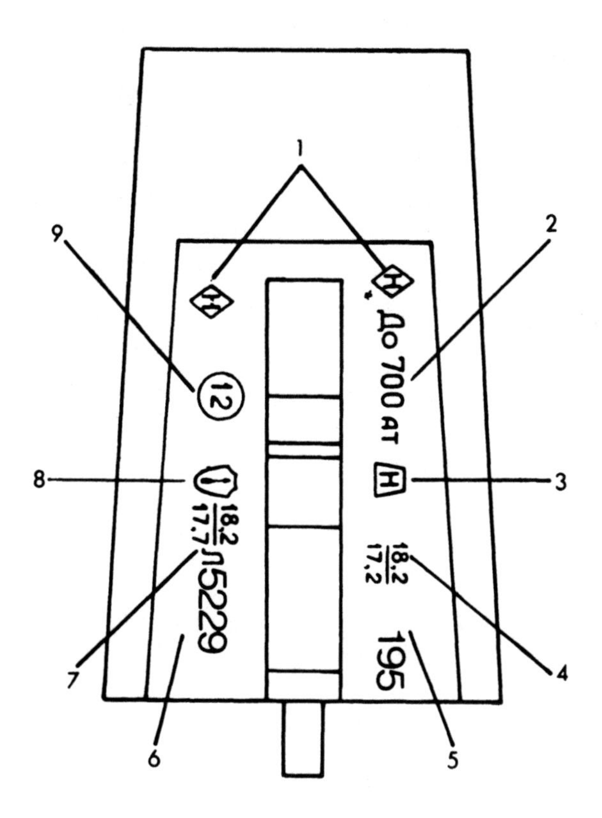
1
2
9
До 700 ат
12
8
3
18,2
17,7
18,2
17,2
Л5229
195
7
4
6
5

SWITZERLAND

The Swiss Gunsmiths Federation, alsways anxious to protect the quality of arms made in Switzerland, originated the inspection mark *(Kontrollstempel)*, and the first chairman of the inspection commission, in 1864, was the famous arms designer, Major Schmidt. Since the Federation was unable to afford its own workshop where guns could be function fired and inspected, Major Schmidt established the first such shop on the premises of the Schweizerischen Industrie-Gesellschaft (SIG) at Neuhausen. It was not until 1871 that the frugal Swiss government decided to establish a proof shop, and this facility was opened toward the end of 1874. Major Schmidt was elected as the first director.

The inspection mark was stamped on a military arm after the arm had been inspected for faultless workmanship and after shooting tests to make certain that the functioning was perfect. The chief inspectors each had their own mark or stamp and it was not until 1943, that the official ordnance inspection stamp was issued to the chief inspector.

 Major Schmidt, 1864–1874.

 Major Werdmüller, 1875–mid–1879.

 Major Vogelsang, 1879–1912.

Major Mühlemann, 1913–1941.

 Captain Hauri, 1942.

 Arms inspection mark, the cross signifies the Federation ordnance examination.

Other inspection marks were used for the acceptance or rejection of parts.

PROOF MARKS

The Swiss military rifle, Model 1889, better known as the Schmidt-Rubin rifle, was the first Swiss military arm to undergo proof firing. The gun was fired with a proof load that produced a pressure 1/3 greater than that of the standard military service round. After the rifle passed proof, this mark was stamped on the receiver. The same mark is in use today.

The Swiss service revolver was not proofed, and proofing of the 7.65 mm Parabellum pistol began only in 1906 with proof loads.

OFFICIAL INSPECTION MARKS

Each single gun part, with a few exceptions, must be inspected carefully for dimensions and quality, and if it passes inspection, the part is marked with a suitable inspection stamp. The location of this inspection mark is determined for each part that passes inspection. Each rejected part is likewise marked, the stamp being placed where the fault was found.

These inspection marks are of a specific size and configuration and each also has the first letter of the inspector's name, as well as the Federation's cross. The reject mark has a reversed „R" before the inspector's initial letter

Acceptance mark for small metal parts.

Acceptance mark for large metal parts. Stamp is hit harder, makes a deeper impression.

Acceptance mark for still larger metal parts – this is a raised mark.

Acceptance mark for wooden components or parts.

Rejection mark for metal parts.

Rejection mark for wooden parts.

The Federation's acceptance marks vary from the above marks.

Acceptance mark and the rejection mark.

GERMAN ORDNANCE CODES

After World War I, Germany was totally disarmed. When Hitler became Reich's Chancellor in 1933, he began an era of re-armament. This had to be done in secrecy, and to conceal what was going on in the German arms and allied industries, manufacturers were assigned code letters or numbers. This ordnance coding began in 1938, continued to the last days of the Third Reich.

Early during WW II, Allied intelligence sources discovered the code, and despite concerted efforts, were unable to break the code. Even after the war when tons of documents were unearthed, the entire list of codes was not found, and thus some of the codes are still unknown.

Manufacturers and sub-contractors were assigned codes, and this coding included not only arms, ammunition, but also binoculars and even saddlebags. In short, anything that the quartermaster of any of the military services required, was coded. There were a few exceptions, but arms collectors are not concerned too much with those exceptions since most of them were marked with the name of the maker.

The system of assigning codes was begun in an orderly fashion, but because of the huge demand for military goods and the constantly increasing number of suppliers and sub-contractors, the orderly system of assigning codes was abandoned and henceforth codes were assigned in a haphazard manner. Some of the codes are well-known to collectors – the Mauser byf, the ac assigned to Walther, the RWS code dnf are readily recognized.

Despite efforts both in Germany and in the United States, by researchers and collectors, the list has never been completed. Some of the manufacturers with unidentified codes were originally producing non-military items, and later produced parts, or did some sub-assembly work, or perhaps branched out into making items needed for the growing military might of Germany. Many of these companies were demolished during the war, others ceased to function, still others are in Communist-occupied areas. It seems reasonable to assume also that some of these concerns would just as soon forget their participation – voluntary or involuntary – in this German debacle.

The beginning collector should not be surprised when he discovers two or even more codes on a gun. Sub-contractors marked the part or parts they made, and each part had to be marked with the maker's code. At first these ordnance codes were numbers but in 1941, the number code was changed to a letter code.

aaa	Waffenfabrik Brünn AG, Prague
aac	Mannesman-Röhrenwerke, Komotau, Sudeten Germany
aak	Waffenfabrik Brünn AG, Prague
aaj	Obenhütten, Vereinigte Oberschlesische Hüttenwerke AG
aak	Waffenwerke Brünn AG, Prague, Wrsoviace plant, Czechoslovakia
aan	Mitteldeutsche Metallwarenfabrik, Erich Frank, Glauchau, Saxony
aar	Geba-Munitions- und Waffenfabrik, Breslau, Czechoslovakia
aaw	Metallwarenfabrik Gebr. Schmidt, Idar-Oberstein
aba	unknown
abb	Friedrichsthaler Eisenwerk, Jennewein & Gapp, Friedrichsthal (Saar)
abc	Deutsche Metallwerke, Weinstraße, Neustadt
abh	Koch & Söhne, Frankenthal-Plomersheim (Iron and metal products)
ac	Carl Walther, Zella-Mehlis, Thuringia
acu	unknown
ad	Patronen-, Zündhütchen- und Metallwarenfabrik AG (formerly Sellier & Bellot), Schönebeck on the Elbe
adc	William Prym, Stollberg, Rheinland
aek	F. Dusek Waffenerzeugung, Oppeln near Nachod, Czechoslovakia
afb	Metabu, Werk Closs, Rauch & Schnitzler, Nürtingen
afu	August Winkhaus, Münster
ai	unknown
aj	unknown
ajf	Junker & Ruh AG, Karlsruhe, Baden
ajn	Union Sprengstoff- und Zündmittelwerke, Alt-Berum
ak	Munitionsfabriken (formerly Sellier & Bellot, Prague), Vlasim, Czechoslovakia

akp Deutsche Röhrenwerke, Poensgen plant, Düsseldorf-Lierenfeld
akv unknown
al Deutsche Leucht- u. Signalwerke, Dr. Feistel AG, Berlin-Charlottenburg
am Otto Eberhardt, Patronenfabrik (Gustloff Co.), Hirtenberg, Austria
ama unknown
amh unknown
amj Waggonfabrik L. Steinfurt, Königsberg
amn Mauser-Werke KG, Neuwied plant
amo Mauser-Werke KG, Waldeck-Kassel plant
amp Dortmund Hoerder Hüttenverein, Dortmund
an Beutemüller & Co., GmbH, Metalwarenfabrik (ammo), Bretten-Baden
and Magdeburger Pumpenfabrik, Otterburg & Co., Magdeburg
anj Kienzle-Uhrenfabrik, Komotau, Sudeten Germany
anx Königs-Laura-Hütte, Königshütte
anz Maschinen- u. Armaturenfabrik, formerly L. Strube, division of Polte, Magdeburg-Buckau
ap Gustloff-Werke, Wuppertal plant, Ronsdorf
apc Continental Caoutchouc Co., GmbH, Hannover
aqe Deutsche Kabelwerke, Berlin
aqk unknown
aqt unknown
aqx Rheinmetall-Borsig, Tegel plant
ar Mauser-Werke, Berlin-Borsigwalde
arb Vereinigte Oberschlesige Hüttenwerke, Andreashütte
arl unknown
asb Deutsche Waffen- u. Munitionsfabriken AG, Berlin-Borsigwalde
aso unknown
asr HAK Hanseatisches-Kettenwerk GmbH, Hamburg-Langenhorn
asx Hösch AG, Dortmund plant
at Klöckner-Werke, Div. Hasper Eisen- u. Stahlwerk
atb Hydrometer AG, Breslau, Czechoslovakia
atl Klöckner-Humbold-Deutz, Ulm

atr	Langbein-Pfannhauser-Werke AG, Leipzig
atw	Mannesman-Röhrenwerke AG, Witten plant, Ruhr
aty	Maschinenfabrik für Massenverpackung, Lübeck-Schlutrup
au	Gute-Hoffnungshütte Oberhausen, Sterkrade plant
auc	Mauser-Werke AG, Cologne-Ehrenfeld
aue	Metall u. Eisen GmbH, Nürnberg
auf	Metall-, Guss- und Presswerk, H. Diehl, Nürnberg
auj	unknown
auu	Patronenhülsen- u. Metalwarenfabrik AG, Rokycany plant, Pilsen, Czechoslovakia
aux	Polte-Werk, Magdeburg
auy	Polte-Werk, Grüneberg
auz	Polte-Werk, Arnstadt
av	Adam Gerhard, Motorenwerke, Oskau Friedrichsdorf, Sudeten Germany
ave	unknown
avk	Ruhrstahl AG, Brackwede-Bielefeld
avm	Rheinhütte GmbH (Formerly Beck & Co.), Wiesbaden
avt	Silva-Metallwerke GmbH, div. of Polte, Genthin
avu	unknown
awj	unknown
awl	Union-Gesellschaft für Metallindustrie, Sils van de Loo u. Co., Werl plant, Fröndenberg, Ruhr
awt	Württembergische Metallwarenfabrik AG, Geislingen (Steige)
ax	unknown
axq	Erfurter Laden Industrie, North Erfurt
axs	Berndorfer Metallwarenfabrik AG, Arthur Krupp, Berndorf, Austria
ay	Alois Pirkel, Elektrotechnische Fabrik
aye	unknown
ayf	Waffenfabrik Erma, B. Geipel GmbH, Erfurt
ayg	unknown
ayk	unknown
aym	unknown, located in Czechoslovakia
ayr	unknown
az	VDM-Halbzeugwerke, Altena
azg	Siemens-Schukert-Werke AG, Berlin
azy	Maschinenfabrik Sangershausen

ba	Sundwiger Messingwerke, Iserlohn, Westphalia
baz	Steyr-Daimler-Puch AG, Steyr, Austria
bb	A. Laue & Co., Berlin
bc	Kupfer- u. Messingwerke KG, Becker & Co., Langenberg, Rheinland
bcd	Wilhelm-Gustloff-Werke, Weimar
bch	unknown
bck	Brüninghaus, Versmold
bcu	Gutehoffnungshütte, Oberhausen
bd	Metallwerke Lange AG, Bodenbach plant, Sudeten Germany
bda	Uhrenfabrik Villingen
bdq	Ehrhardt & Kirsten, Koffer- u. Lederwarenfabrik, Leipzig
bdr	Richard Ehrhardt, Lederwarenfabrik, Poeseneck, Thuringia
bdy	Pittner, Leipzig
be	Berndorfer Metallwarenfabrik, Arthur Krupp AG, Berndorf, Austria
bed	Gustloff-Werke, Weimar
beh	Ernst Leitz GmbH, Wetzlar
bej	Maschinenfabrik Wolf, Buckau
bek	Hensoldt-Werk für Optik und Mechanik, Herborn
bf	Deutsche Röhrenwerke AG, Mühlheim, Ruhr
bfn	New York-Hamburger Gummifabrik
bg	Enzesfelder Metallwerke, Vienna, Austria
bh	Brünner Waffenfabrik AG, Brünn, Czechoslovakia
bj	Niebecker & Schumacher, Iserlohn, Westphalia
bjm	Klöckner Werke, Deutz plant
bjv	Böhmisch-Mährische Kolben-Danek AG, Vysocan plant, Prague
bk	Metall-, Walz- u. Plattierwarenfabrik Hinrichs & Auffermann AG, Wuppertal
bkp	Gewehrfabrik Burgsmüller & Söhne GmbH, Kreiensen
bkq	Johannes Suremann GmbH, Röhrenfabrik, Arnsberg
bky	Böhmische Waffenfabrik AG, Prague, Ung.-Bro plant. Moravia, Czechoslovakia
bkz	unknown
bl	unknown
bla	E. G. Leuner GmbH, Bautzen
blc	Carl Zeiss, Military Division, Jena

bln	unknown
blp	Burgsmüller & Sohn, Kreiensen
blr	unknown
blu	Sprengstoffwerke, Blumenau near Felixdorf
blx	unknown
bm	unknown
bmb	Metallwarenfabrik Binder, Reichertshofen
bmd	Max G. Müller, Fabrik für Lederwaren & Heeresbedarf, Nürnberg
bmf	Berndorfer Metallwarenfabrik, Berndorf, Austria
bmj	Hensoldt & Söhne, Mechanisch-Optische Werke AG, Wetzlar
bml	unknown
bmu	Carl Kuntze, Sattlerwarenfabrik, Penig, Saxony
bmv	Rheinmetall-Borsig AG, Sömmerda plant, Sömmerda
bmz	Minerva-Nähmaschinenfabrik AG, Boskowitz, Czechoslovakia
bn	unknown
bnd	Maschinenfabrik Augsburg-Nürnberg, Nürnberg plant, Nürnberg
bne	Metallwarenfabrik Odertal GmbH, Odertal
bnf	Polte, contract plant, Wolfenbüttel
bnz	Steyr-Daimler-Puch AG, Steyr, Austria
bo	unknown
boa	Venditor, Troisdorf
bod	Venditor, Troisdorf
bot	Metallwerke Neheim
bp	unknown
bpd	Optische Anstalt O. P. Görz, Vienna, Austria
bpr	Johannes Grossfuss, Metall- u. Locierwarenfabrik, Döbeln, Saxony
bpt	unknown
bq	unknown
bqo	Krupp-Gruson, Magdeburg-Buckau
bqs	Oderhütte Kürstin
bqt	Eugen Müller, Pyrotechnische Fabrik, Vienna, Austria
br	Mathias Bäuerle, Laufwerke GmbH, St. Georgen, Black Forest

brb	unknown
brd	Hagenuk, Neufeldt & Kuhnke GmbH, Kiel
brg	unknown
bsv	Tönshoff, Horn in Lippe
bt	unknown
bte	unknown
btk	Aluminium-Werke Honsel, Werdohl
btn	unknown
buc	Metallwerke Windelsbleiche near Bielefeld
buh	Röchling, Wetzlar
bv	unknown
bvl	Theodor Bergmann & Co., Abteilung Automaten- & Metallwarenfabrikation, Hamburg-Altona
bvv	unknown
bw	unknown
bwc	Maschinenfabrik Brackwede
bwn	Krupp-Stahlwerk u. Maschinenfabrik, Essen
bwo	Rheinmetall-Borig AG, Düsseldorf
bwp	Berlin-Anhaltische-Maschinenbau AG, Dessau
bwq	unknown
bwr	Werk Lauchhammer
bwx	Ruhrstahl, Henrichshütte, Hattingen
bxb	Skoda-Werke, Pilsen, Czechoslovakia
bxe	Bochumer Verein
bxm	Vereinigte Zünder- u. Kabelwerke, Meissen
bxn	unknown, Czechoslovakia
by	unknown
byc	Brückenbauanstalt August Klonne AG, Dortmund
bye	Hanomag, Hannover
byf	Mauser-Werke, Oberndorf on the Neckar
byg	Johann Wyksen, Optische u. Feinmaschinen, Katowitz, Poland
bym	Genossenschafts-Maschinenhaus der Büchsenmacher, Ferlach, Austria
byq	Pohlmann & Co., Hammerwerke, Wetterburg, Hessen-Nassau
byr	Ruhrstahl, Witten-Annen
bys	Ruhrstahl, Witten

byw	Johann Schäfer, Stettiner Schraubenwerk, Stettin
bzt	Fritz Wolf, Gewehrfabrik, Zella-Mehlis, Thuringia
bzz	unknown
ca	Vereinigte Deutsche Nickelwerke, Schwerte, Ruhr
cag	Swarowski, D., Glasfabrik u. Tyrolit, Wattens, Tyrol, Austria
cau	unknown
cbl	VDM-Halbwerkzeuge, Nürnberg branch
cbr	Böhlerwerk, Böhler & Co., Waidhofen, Austria
cby	Schöller-Bleckmann, Ternitz, Niederdonau
ccb	Stahlwerke Brünninghaus AG, Westhofen, Westphalia
ccd	DEMAG, Wetter
ccx	Optische u. Feinmaschinenwerke, Hugo Meyer & Co., Görlitz
cdc	Kern, Klager & Co., Lederwaren, Berlin
cdg	Auwärter & Bubeck KG, Lederwarenfabrik, Stuttgart
cdo	Theodor Bergmann & Co., Waffen- u.Munitionsfabrik, Velten plant, Velten on the Main
cdp	Theodor Bergmann & Co., Waffen- u. Munitionsfabrik, Bernau plant, Berlin
cdv	Metallwarenfabrik Ludwig Maybaum, Sundern, Westphalia
ce	Sauer & Sohn, Waffenfabrik, Suhl, Thuringia
cey	Karl Budischovsky & Söhne, Österreichische Lederindustrie AG, Vienna
cf	Westfälische Anhaltische Sprengstoff AG, Oranienburg plant
cg	Finower Industrie GmbH, Finow, Mark
cgn	Rohrbacher Lederfabrik, Josef Pöschels Söhne, Rohrbach
cgt	unknown
ch	Fabrique Nationale d'Armes de Guerre, Herstal, Liege, Belgium
chd	Deutsche Industrie-Werke AG, Berlin-Spandau
chh	DEW, Hannover plant, Linden
cja	unknown
cjg	unknown
cjn	Uhrenfabrik, Gebr. Junghans, Schramberg, Black Forest
ck	Metallwerk Neumeyer, Munich
ckc	Deutsche Eisenwerke AG, Mühlheim, Ruhr
ckl	Eisen- u. Hüttenwerke, Thale, Harz

cko	Hüttenwerk, Eisengiesserei u. Maschinenfabrik, Michelstadt, Odenwald
cl	Metschke Karl, Auto- u. Maschinenreparatur, Berlin plant
clg	unknown
cma	unknown
cmg	Metallwarenfabrik Halver, Peter W. Haurand GmbH, Halver, Westphalia
cms	Konrad Lindhorst, Berlin
cmw	Dr. Ing. Rudolf Hell, Berlin
cmz	Zünderwerke Ernst Brün, Krefeld, Linn
cnd	Krupp-National-Registrierkassen (cash registers) GmbH, Berlin plant
cob	Netzschkauer Maschinenfabrik, Stark & Söhne, Netzschkau, Saxony
coe	Lübecker Maschinenbau-Gesellschaft
cof	Waffenfabrik Eickhorn, Solingen
con	Franz Stock, Maschinen- u. Werkzeugfabrik, Berlin
cos	Gebrüder Merz, Merz-Werke, Frankfurt, Main
cow	Wintershall AG, Spritzgusswerk, Berlin
cpj	unknown
cpn	Werk Apolda
cpo	Rheinmetall-Borsig AG, Berlin-Marienfeld
cpp	Rheinmetall-Borsig AG, Breslau plant
cpq	Rheinmetall-Borsig AG, Gubeb plant
cq	Warz & Co., Zella-Mehlis, Thuringia
cdq	unknown
cr	unknown
crm	PhyWE, Göttingen
cro	R. Fuess, Optische Industrie, Berlin-Steglitz
crs	Paul Weyersberg & Co., Waffenfabrik, Solingen
crv	Fritz Werner, Plant II, Berlin
crw	Maschinenfabrik Hofmann GmbH, Breslau
csa	Skoda Werke
csq	Pollux, Ludwigshafen, Rhein
csx	Gothaer Metallwarenfabrik GmbH
cte	Klöckner Maschinenfabrik, Manstadt division, Troisdorf
ctf	Eisenwerke Gaggenau GmbH, Gaggenau, Baden
ctg	Karlshütte Waldenburg, Altwasser, Silesia

ctn Freidricks & Co., Hanseatische Werkstätten für Feinmechanik u. Optik

cts Märkische Werke, H. Hillmann GmbH, drop forge plant, Halver

ctu unknown

cty unknown

cue Röchling-Buderus-Stahlwerke, Finofurt plant, Brandenburg

cuf Röchling-Buderus-Stahlwerke, Melle plant, Hannover

cuy unknown

cuz Eisenwerk Maximilianhütte, stamping plant, Thuringia, Unterwellenborn

cva Eisenwerke Maximilianhütte, iron mongery division, Fronberg

cvb Otto Sindel, Lederwarenfabrik, Berlin

cvc Zeschke Nachf. Gebr. L. Zeuschner, Koffer- und Lederwarenfabrik, Müllrose near Frankfurt on the Oder

cvg VDM, Frankfurt-Hedderheim

cvl WKC Waffenfabrik, Solingen Wald

cvs Paul Weyersberg & Co., Waffenfabrik, Solingen

cvv Maschinenfabrik B. Holthaus, Dinklage (Vechte/Old.)

cwb Brandenburger Eisenwerke

cwg Westfälisch-Anhaltische Sprengstoff AG, Coswig plant

cww Karl Weiss, Lederwarenfabrik, Braunschweig

cxa Ruhrstahl AG, Stahlwerk Krieger, Düsseldorf-Oberhausen

cxb Moll, Lederwarenfabrik, Goch, Rheinland

cxd Maschinenfabrik Becker & Co., Magdeburg

cxe unknown

cxg Metallwarenfabrik Spreewerk AG, Berlin-Spandau

cxh Kienzle, Schwenningen on the Neckar

cxm Gustav Genschow & Co., Berlin

cxn Emil Busch AG, Optische Industrie, Rathenow

cxq Spreewerke GmbH, Metallwarenfabrik, Berlin-Spandau

cxw unknown

cyd Nottebohm, Lüdenscheid

cyh Hüttenwerke Siegerland, rolling mills, Eichner

cyq Metallwarenfabrik Spreewerk, Berlin-Spandau

cyw unknown

czf Maschinenfabrik Steubing & Co., Berlin

czm Gustav Genschow & Co., AG, Berlin
czn Emil Busch AG, Optische Industrie, Rathenow
czo Heereszeugamt, Geschoßwerkstatt, Königsberg
czq Schichau-Elbing, Königsberg division
czs Brennabor Werke AG, Brandenburg
dah Junkers, Dessau
dar Metallindustrie Schönbeck AG, Schönbeck on the Elbe
daz Maximilinahütte, plant II, Unterwellenborn, Thuringia
dbg Dynamit AG, Düneberg plant (formerly Alfred Nobel & Co.)
dbh Mannesmann, Düsseldorf plant, Rath
dbk unknown
dc unknown
dde Robert Larsen, Fabrik für Leder u. Stoffwaren, Berlin
ddt unknown
ddx Voigtländer u. Sohn AG, Braunschweig
de unknown
dea Frankfurter Maschinenbau, Pokorny & Wittekind, Frankfurt
dec Bleiwerk Goslar
dej unknown
dev DEW, Remscheid plant
dfb Gustloff Co., Waffenfabrik, Suhl
dgb Dynamit AG, Düneberg plant (formerly A. Nobel & Co.)
dgl Remo Gewehrfabrik, Gebr. Rempt, Suhl
dgz Böhler, Kapfenberg, Austria
dha Krupp, Hannover plant
dbn unknown
dhp H. Burgsmüller, Gewehrfabrik, Kreiensen-Harz
djf Draht-Bremer, Rostock, Mecklenburg
dkk Friedrich Offermann & Söhne, Lederwarenfabrik, Bensberg
dla Karl Barth, Militäreffekten-Fabrik, Waldbrohl, Rheinland
dld Kromag, Hirtenberg, Austria
dlu Ewald Lünenschloss, Militäreffekten-Fabrik, Solingen
dma Heeresmunitionsanstalt u. Geschoßwerkstatt, Zeithain
dmk Ilseder Hütte, rolling mill, Peiner
dmo Auto-Union, Chemnitz, Czechoslovakia
dms unknown
dmy Fritz Werner, Berlin-Marienfeld
dn Vereinigte Deutsche Nickelwerke, Laband, Upper Silesia

dna unknown
dnb unknown
dnf Rheinische-Westfälische Sprengstoff AG, Stadeln plant near Nürnberg
dnh Rheinische-Westfälische Sprengstoff AG, Durlach plant, Baden
dnv unknown
dnz Schwarzwälder Apparatenbauanstalt, August Schwek & Söhne, Villingen, Black Forest
dom Westfälische Metallindustrie, Lippstadt
dot Waffenwerke Brünn, Brünn plant, Czechoslovakia
dou Waffenwerke Brünn, Bystrica, Czechoslovakia
dov Waffenwerke Brünn, Vsetin plant, Czechoslovakia
dow Waffenwerke Brünn, Prerau plant, Czechoslovakia
dox Waffenwerke Brünn, Podbrezova plant, Czechoslovakia
dpf unknown
dph I.G. Farbenindustrie AG, Autogen plant, Frankfurt
dpk Hagenuk, Berlin-Tempelhof
dpl Remo Gewehrfabrik, Gebr. Rempt, Suhl
dpm Poldi-Hütte, Komotau, Sudeten Germany
dps Auto-Union, Mittweida, Saxony
dpu Schlothauer, GmbH, Metallwaren, Ruhla
dpv Zeiss-Ikon, Dresden
dpw Zeiss-Ikon, Görz plant, Berlin-Zehlendorf
dpx Zeiss-Ikon, Stuttgart
drh unknown
drv HASAG, Tschenstochau
drz unknown
dsb unknown
dsh Ing. F. Janecek, Gewehrfabrik, Prague
dsj WAMA Metallwerke, Oberlungwitz, Saxony
dsx Röchling-Buderus, Wetzlar
dta A. Waldhausen, Inh. M. Bruchmann, Sattler u. Kofferfabrik, Cologne
dtf unknown
dtu G. J. Ensink & Co., Spezialfabrik für Militärausrüstung, Ohrdruf, Thuringia
dtv C. Otto Gehrckens, Leder- u. Riemenwerke, Pinneberg

dun	Poldi Hütte, Kladno plant, Czechoslovakia
dut	unknown
duv	Berliner-Lübecker Maschinenfabrik, Lübeck plant
dvc	unknown
dvr	Johann Pröhlich, Lederwarenfabrik, Vienna
dvu	Schichau, Elbing
dvw	unknown
dwc	unknown
dwm	Deutsche Waffen- und Munitionswerke, Berlin-Borsigwalde
dxs	Thyssen, Duisburg-Hamborn
dye	Ed. Pitschmann, Pyrotechnik, Innsbruck, Austria
dym	Runge & Kaulfuss, Rathenow
dyq	DEW, Werdohl plant
dza	Bleiwerke Dr. Schülcke, Hamburg
dzl	Optische Anstalt Oigee, Berlin
dzw	Metallwerke v. Galkowsky & Kielblock, Finow
eaf	Mechanoptik-Gesellschaft für Präzisionstechnik, Aude & Reipe, Babelsberg
eah	Brüninghaus, Werdohl
eak	Deutsche Werke Kiel
ean	Eisen- u. Metallwerke, Lippstadt
eba	Scharfenberg & Teubert GmbH, Metallwarenfabrik, Breitungen
ebd	unknown
ebf	Hüttenwerke Siegerland, Charlottenhütte plant, Wiederschelden
ebk	unknown
eca	unknown
ecc	Oskar Lunig, Pyrotechnische Fabrik, Möhringen
ecd	Graf Lippold, Pyrotechnische Fabrik, Wuppertal-Elberfeld
ecv	unknown
edg	J. A. Henckels, Zwillingswerke, Solingen
edk	Auto-Union, Zschoppau plant, Saxony
edq	Deutsche Waffen- u. Munitionswerke AG, Lübeck-Schlutrup
edr	unknown
eds	Zündapp, Nürnberg
edw	unknown
edy	unknown

edz	unknown
eec	unknown
eed	Gewehr- u. Fahrradteilfabrik H. Weirauch, Zella-Mehlis
eef	unknown
eeg	Hermann Weirauch, Gewehr- u. Fahrradteilfabrik, Zella-Mehlis
eeh	unknown
eej	Märkisches Walzwerk, Staußberg, district Potsdam
eek	unknown
eel	Metallwarenfabrik Wissner, Brotterode plant
eem	Selve-Kornbiegel, Dornheim AG, Munitionsfabrik, Sömmerda, Saxony
eeo	Deutsche Waffen- u. Munitionsfabriken AG, Posen plant
eet	unknown
eeu	unknown
eev	unknown
eey	Metallwarenfabrik Treuenbrietzen GmbH, Röderhof plant
egy	Ing. Fr. August Pfeffer, Oberlind, Thuringia
eh	unknown
eky	Volkswagenwerk, Wolfsburg
elg	WASAG, Elsnig plant
emh	unknown
emj	Adalbert Fischer, Berlin
emp	Dynamit AG (formerly Alfred Nobel & Co.), Empelde plant
emq	Karl Zeiss, Jena
emu	Mathe Uhrenfabrik, Schwenningen
enc	unknown
enz	Enzesfelder Metallwerk, Enzesfeld plant, Vienna
eom	H. Huck, Metallwarenfabrik, Nürnberg
eov	unknown
eox	unknown
epf	unknown
eqf	Karl Bocker, Lederwarenfabrik, Waldbrohl, Rheinland
erg	A. Doppert, Treibriemenfabrik (driving belt mfr.), Kitzingen
erm	unknown
erv	unknown
eso	Optische Werke G. Rodenstock, Munich
etb	Steubing & Co., Graslitz, Sudeten, Germany

etl	unknown
ety	unknown
eue	Otto Reichel, Inh. Rudolf Fischer, Lederwarenfabrik, Lengfeld, Erzgebirge
eug	Optische Präzisionswerke GmbH, Warsaw, Poland
euh	unknown
eun	unknown
euo	unknown
evv	unknown
evz	unknown
ews	Skodawerke, Königsgrätz plant, Czechoslovakia
ewx	Franz u. Karl Vögels, Lederwarenfabrik, Cologne
exd	Auto-Union, Audi plant
exp	Hans Kollmorgen, Optische Anstalt, Berlin
exq	unknown
exs	Skodawerke, Königgrätz, Czechoslovakia
exw	Metallwerke Holleischen, Kreis Mies, Sudeten Germany
exx	unknown
eyd	unknown
fa	Mansfeld AG, Hettstedt, Südharz
faa	Deutsche Waffen- u. Munitionsfabriken AG, Karlsruhe
fb	Mansfeld AG, Rothenburg plant, Saale
fc	Mansfeld AG, Alstedt plant, Thuringia
fck	unknown
fco	Sendlinger Optische Glaswerke GmbH, Berlin-Zehlendorf
fcv	unknown
fd	Stolberger Metallwerke AG (formerly Asten, Lynen & Schleicher), Stolberg
fde	Dynamit AG (formerly A. Nobel & Co.), Förde plant
fe	unknown
fee	Augsburger Waagenfabrik, Ludwig Pfisterer, Augsburg
feh	unknown
fer	Metallwerke Wandhofen, Schwerte, Westphalia
feu	unknown
ffo	unknown
fko	unknown
fkx	Gustav Sudbrack, Lederwaren u. Gamaschenfabrik, Bielefeld
flp	unknown

fnh	Böhmische Waffenfabrik, Strkonitz plant, Prague
fnk	unknown
fnq	unknown
fpx	Schäffer & Budenberg, Magdeburg-Buckau
fqn	Vereinigte Leichtmetallwerke, Hannover-Linden
fra	Draht- und Metallwarenfabrik GmbH, Salzwedel
frp	Stahlwerke Harkot-Eicken, Hagen, Westphalia
fsx	Albin Scholle, Lederwarenfabrik, Zeitz
ftc	Frost & Jahnel, Breslau, Czechoslovakia
ftf	unknown
fue	Skodawerke, machine shop, Dubnica plant, Czechoslovakia
fuu	Strube GmbH, subsidiary of Polte, Magdeburg
fva	Draht- u. Metallwarenfabrik GmbH, Salzwedel
fwh	Norddreutsche Maschinenfabrik GmbH, main office, Berlin
fwr	Optische Anstalt Sallfeld GmbH, Saalfeld
fwz	Eisen- u. Emaillierwerke Wilhelmshütte (iron and enamel works), Sprottau-Wilhelmshütte
fxa	Eisenacher Karosseriewerke Assman GmbH, Eisenach (chassis plant)
fxo	C. G. Haenel, Waffen- u. Fahrradfabrik, Suhl
fxp	Hans Kollmorgen, Optische Anstalt, Berlin
fyd	Skodawerke, Adamsthal plant
fze	Waffenfabrik Höller, Solingen
fzs	Waffenfabrik Heinrich Krieghoff, Suhl
ga	Hirsch, Kupfer- u. Messingwerk AG, Finow
gal	unknown
gaq	Otto Stephan, Leder- u. Lederwarenfabrik, Mühlhausen
gau	Sudhaus & Söhne, Iserlohn
gb	Vereinigte N. Werke, Schwerte
gbc	unknown
gbd	unknown
gbv	Witte & Co., Velbert
gcd	unknown
gcw	Göhring-Hebenstreit, Radebeul near Dresden
gcx	Karl Brettschneider, Mähr.-Schönberg
gcy	unknown
geu	Kuhbier & Co., Präzisionspreßstücke (precision stampings), Wipperfürth

gfg	Karl Hepting & Co., Leder- u. Gürtelfabrik, Stuttgart
ggb	I. G. Königshütte u. Laurahütte Kattowitz, main office, Röchling, Königshütte, OS
ggk	unknown
ghf	Fritz Kiess & Co., GmbH, Waffenfabrik, Suhl
ghp	Ruf & Co., Optische Werke Kassel, Hessen-Nassau
ghx	unknown
gil	Auto-Union, Spandau plant
gjd	unknown
gjh	Rudolf Conte, Nachf. Theodor Seibold, Fabrik für Lederwaren, Offenbach on the Main
gjk	unknown
gk	Mansfeld AG, Hettstedt, Südharz
gmo	Rahm & Kampmann, Lederwarenfabrik, Kaiserslautern plant
gn	Aug. Wellner, Aue, Saxony
gon	unknown
gpe	unknown
gpt	nunknown
gqm	unknown
grk	unknown
grz	Gebr. Kruger, Lederwarenfabrik, Breslau, Czechoslovakia
gsb	Rheinmetall-Borsig, branch-office Liege, operated by Loewen (formerly S. A. des Ateliers de la Dyle)
gsc	S.A. Belge des Mecanique et de L'Armement, Monceau-sur-Sambre, Belgium
gtb	J. F. Eisfeld GmbH, Pulver- u. Pyrotechnische Fabriken, Güntersberge plant
gug	Ungarische Optische Werke AG, Budapest, Hungary
guj	Werner D. Kühn, Optische Industrie, Berlin-Steglitz
gum	Bergisch-Märkische Eisenwerke, Velbert, Rheinland
gut	Walter Schurmann & Co., Lederwarenfabrik, Bielefeld
guy	Werkzeugmaschinenfabrik Oelikon, Bührle & Co., Zurich, Schwitzerland
gvj	Ruhrstahl AG, Gelsenkirchen
gvm	unknown
gxx	unknown
gxy	Klinge, Lederwarenfabrik, Dresden-Lobtau
gyf	DEW, Bochum plant

gyo	Hans Dinkelmaeyer, Lederwarenfabrik, Nürnberg
gyu	unknown
gyx	unknown
gyy	unknown
gyz	unknown
gzf	Westfälische Eisen- u. Blechwarenwerke, Siegen
ha	Treuenbrietzen Metallwarenfabrik GmbH, Sebaldushof plant
ham	Dynamit AG (formerly A. Nobel & Co.), Hamm plant
has	Pulverfabrik Hasloch, Hasloch on the Main
hbg	Alfred Schwarz AG, Metallwerk Frödenburg on the Ruhr, Eisenach plant
hbu	Heinrich List, Elektrotechnik u. Mechanik, Teltow & Steglitz
hck	Georg A. Lerch GmbH, Lederwaren u. Stanzwerk (leather goods and stamping), Mettman, Rheinland
hdk	unknown
hdt	Märkischer Metallbau, Oranienburg
hdv	Optische Werke Osterrode GmbH, Osterrode, Harz
hen	unknown
hew	Ing. F. Janecek, Waffenwerke, Prague
hft	Becker & Co., GmbH, Militär- u. Feuerwehrausrüstungen (military and firefighting equipment), Berlin
hgs	W. Gustav Burmeister, Pyrotechnische Fabrik u. Signalmittelwerk (fireworks and pyrotechnics), Hamburg
hgu	unknown
hhc	Union Gesellschaft f. Metallindustrie, Sils van de Loo & Co., Frödenberg plant
hhg	Rheinmetall-Borsig AG, Tegel plant
hhj	unknown
hhr	unknown
hhu	Metallwarenfabrik Schmalkalden
hhv	Steyr-Daimler-Puch AG, Nibelungen plant, St. Valentin, Austria
hhw	Metallwerke Silberhütte GmbH, Andreasberg, Harz
hhx	unknown
hhy	unknown
hhz	Röchlingwerke, Völklingen
hjg	Kimmach & Brunn, Fabrik für Heeresausrüstung, Kaiserslautern

hjh	Karl Ackva, Lederfabrik, Bad Kreuznach
hkm	Karl Braun AG, Optische Industrie, Nürnberg
hla	Metallwarenfabrik Treuenbrietzen GmbH, Sebaldushof plant
hlb	Metallwarenfabrik Treuenbrietzen GmbH, Selterhof plant
hlc	Zieh- u. Stanzwerk (wire pulling and stamping), Schleusingen
hld	Metallwarenfabrik Treuenbrietzen GmbH, Belsig plant
hle	Metallwarenfabrik Treuenbrietzen GmbH, Röderhof plant
hlu	unknown
hlv	Maury & Co., Lederwarenfabrik, Offenbach on the Main
hly	unknown
hnx	Walter KG, Kiel, Kiel plant and Tannenberg plant
hre	unknown
hrk	unknown
hrl	unknown
hrn	Preßwerk Metgethen, East Prussia
hta	unknown
htg	Polte Armaturen- u. Maschinenfabriken AG, Duderstadt plant, Westphalia
htl	unknown
htq	Junghanswerke, Schwenningen plant
hwd	Westfälische-Anhaltische Sprengstoff AG, Herrenwald plant
i	Astra-Werke, Chemnitz
j	unknown
ja	Schmöle, Menden
jan	Deutsche Versuchsanstalt für Luftfahrt, Berlin-Adlerhof
jba	A. Wunderlich Nachf., Fabrik für Heeresausrüstung (factory for military equipment), Berlin-Neukölln
jfp	Dr. Karl Leiss, Optische Mechanische Instrumente, Berlin-Steglitz
jfs	Junkers, Magdeburg division
jhg	Gustav Genschow & Co., AG, Lederwarenfabriken, Alstadt-Hachenburg
jhv	Metallwaren, Waffen- und Maschinenfabrik AG, Budapest Hungary
jkg	Königl. Ungar. Staatliche Eisen-, Stahl- u. Maschinenfabrik, Budapest
jkh	Karl Busse, Ausrüstungsgegenstände (equipment), Mainz
jlj	Heereszeugamt Ingolstadt

jln	Deutsche Lederwerkstätten GmbH, Pirmasens
jme	Armeemarinehaus Berlin, Berlin-Charlottenburg
jmh	unknown
jnh	Hensoldt Werke für Optik u. Mechanik, Herborn, Dillkreis
jnk	Conti, Hannover
jnw	Eisenwerk Steele, Essen-Steele
joa	Dresdner Koffer- u. Taschenfabrik, Karl Heinichen, Dresden
jrr	Junghans, Renchen plant, Baden
jrs	Junghans, branch office, Vienna
jry	Hermann Herold, Olberhain
jsd	Gustav Reinhard, Lederwarenfabrik, Berlin
jse	Metallwerke Zöblitz AG, Zöblitz
jtb	S.A. Tavaro, Ghent, Belgium
jtt	unknown
jua	Danuvia Waffen- u. Munitionsfabriken AG, Budapest, Hungary
jut	Vereinigte Wiener Metallwerke, Vienna
jvb	unknown
jvd	unknown
jve	Optische Werke Ernst Ludwig, Weixdorf, Anhalt, Saxony
jvf	Wilhelm Brand, Treibriemenfabrik (driving belt factory), Heidelberg
jwa	Moritz Stecher, Lederwerk, Freiburg
jwh	Manufacture d'Armes Chatellerault, Chatellerault, France
k	Firma Luch & Wagner, Suhl
ka	Gerhardi & Co., Lüdenscheid, Westphalia
kam	Hasag, Eisen- u. Metallwerke GmbH, Skarzysko Kamienna
kaw	unknown
kbg	Erwin Backhaus, Remscheid
kce	Schneider & Co., Le Creuot, France
kdj	unknown
keb	Manufacture d'Armes Nationale de Levallois, Paris
kfa	Staatliches Arsenal, Sarajevo, Yougoslavia
kfb	unknown
kfg	Staatliches Arsenal, Sarajevo, Yugoslavia
kfk	Dansk Industrie Syndicat, Copenhagen, Denmark
kjj	Askania Werke AG, Berlin-Friedenau
kjl	unknown

kkd	Wilhelm Stern, Lederwarenfabrik, Posen
kkn	unknown
klb	J. F. Eisfeld GmbH, Kieselbach plant
kle	Steyr-Daimler-Puch AG, Warsaw plant, Poland
klg	Przemot, Präzisions Metallverarbeitung, Litzmannstadt
kls	Steyr-Daimler-Puch AG, Warsaw plant, Poland
koz	unknown
kgd	Junghans, Montagestelle, Exbrücke, Elsaß
krd	Lignose Sprengstoffwerke GmbH, Kriewald
krg	Emil Busch AG, Optische Werke, Budapest
krj	Messerschmidt, Augsburg
krl	Dynamit AG (formerly Alfred Nobel & Co.), Krümmel plant, Koblenz
krq	Emil Busch AG, Optische Werke, Rathenow, Brandenburg
kru	Lignose Sprengstoffwerke GmbH, Kruppsmühle plant
kry	Lignose Sprengstoffwerke GmbH, Kruppsmühle plant
ksb	Manufacture Nationale d'Armes de Levallois, Levallois, Paris
ksm	Junghans, Braunau plant, Sudeten Germany
ktz	Deutsche Sprengchemie, Klietz plant
kum	J. F. Eisfeld, Pulver- u. Pyrotechnische Fabrik GmbH
kun	Lignose Sprengstoffwerk, Kunigunde plant
kur	Steyr-Daimler-Puch AG, Warsaw plant, Poland
kus	unknown
kvu	Lignose Sprengstoffwerk GmbH, Kruppsmühle plant
kwe	Gamma Feinmechanik u. Optik, Budapest
kwn	S.A. Fiat, Turin, Italy
kye	Intreprinderile Metalurgie, Pumitra Voina Societate, Anonima Romana, Fabrica de Armament, Brasov, Romania
kyn	Astra, Fabrica Romana de Vagone, Motoaene Armament si Munitione, Brasov, Romania
kyo	Intreprinderile Metalurgie, Pumitra Voina Aocietate, Anonima Romana, Fabrica de Armament, Brasov, Romania
kyp	Rumänisch-Deutsche Industrie u. Handels AG, Budapest
kza	Mauser-Werke, Karlsruhe
kzn	Kienzle, Dammerkirch plant
kzu	unknown
la	Dürener Metallwerke, Düren
lac	Zuchthaus (penitentiary) Coswig, Anhalt

lae	Heinrich Zeiss, Gastingen
lax	Lennewerk Altena
ldb	Deutsche Pyrotechnische Fabriken GmbH, Berlin plant, Malchow
ldc	Deutsche Pyrotechnische Fabriken GmbH, Cleebronn plant
ldn	Deutsche Pyrotechnische Fabriken GmbH, Neumarkt plant, Oberpfalz
ldo	unknown
lge	Kugelfabrik Schulte & Co., Tente, Rheinland
lgs	unknown
ljp	unknown
lkc	unknown
lkm	Munitionsfabriken (formerly Sellier & Bellot), Veitsberg plant, Prague
lmg	Karl Zeiss, Jena
lpk	unknown
ltm	Metallwarenfabrik Litzmannstadt
lwg	Optische Werke Osterrode GmbH, Freiheit near Osterrode
lww	Huet & Cie., Paris
lwx	O.P.L. Optique et Precision de Levallois, Levallois, Paris
lwy	Societe Optique et Mechanique de Haute Precision, Paris
lyf	Metallurgia Werke AG, Radomsko, Poland
lza	Mauser-Werke AG, Karlsruhe plant
ma	Metallwerke Lange AG, Aue, Saxony
mdr	Vereinigte Leichtmetallwerke, Bonn
mhk	Metallwerke Schwarzwald AG, Villingen
mhv	Finow Kupfer- u. Messingwerke AG, Finow
mjr	Union Gesellschaft für Met. Ind., Sils van de Loo & Co., Thorn plant
mkf	Trierer Walzwerk, Wuppertal-Langerfeld
ml	unknown
mnf	VDM Heddernheim, Frankfurt on the Main
mng	VDM Heddernheim, Frankfurt on the Main
moc	Johan Springer's Erben, Gewehrfabrikanten, Vienna
mog	Deutsche Sprengchemie, Moschweig plant
moo	Klöckner-Werke AG, Düsseldorf plant
moz	Eisenwerk Gesellschaft Maximilianhütte, Maxhütte-Haidhof
mpp	Metallwerk K. Leibfried, Böblingen, Sindelfingen plant

mpr	S.A. Hispano Suiza, Geneva, Switzerland
mpu	unknown
mpv	Schmolz u. Bickenbach, Neuss plant, Düsseldorf
mpy	Klöckner-Werke AG, Georgsmarienhütte Osnabrück
mrb	Skodawerke, Prague plant, Smichow
mrd	Hüttenwerke Siegerland, Wissen
mrf	Fr. Krupp, Berthawerk AG, Breslau
mws	Munitionswerke Schönebeck
myx	Rheinmetall-Borsig AG, Sömmerda plant
na	Westfälische Kupfer- u. Messingwerke AG, Lüdenscheid, Westphalia
nas	Uhrenfabrik Junghans, Schramberg, Black Forest
nb	Waffenfabrik Kongsberg, Norway
nbe	Hasag, Eisen- u. Metallwerke GmbH, Tachenstocha plant
nbh	Walther Steiner, Eisenkonstruktionen (iron construction), Suhl
nbr	Metallwarenfabrik Hubert Prünte, Neheim-Hüsten
ncr	Krupp-Germaniawerft, Kiel-Gaarden
ndn	Balkan Country under German occupation
ndr	Krupp Essen
nea	Walther Steiner, Eisenkonstruktionen, Suhl
nec	Waffenwerke Brünn AG, V Gurein plant, Prague
ned	Krupp, Essen
nfw	unknown
nfx	Rheinisch-Westfälische Munitionsfabriken GmbH, plants in Warsaw and Prague
ngk	Dr. Grasse
nhr	Rheinmetall-Borsig AG, Sömmerda plant
nmn	Königs- u. Bismarckhütte AG, Walzwerk Bismarckhütte-OS (rolling mill)
nn	unknown
nrh	unknown
ntf	unknown
nwk	Heinrich List, Rheinau, Elsaß
nxc	unknown
nxr	Anschütz & Co., Kiel-Neumühlen
nyv	Rheinmetall-Borsig AG, Unterlass plant
nyw	Gustloff-Werke, Otto Eberhard, Meinigen plant

oa	Eduard Hück, Metallwalzwerk, Lüdenscheid
oao	Anschütz, Kiel-Neumühlen
obn	Hagenuk, Reichenbach plant
ocw	Heinrich List, Berlin-Steglitz
odg	Deutsche Sprengchemie, Oderberg plant
oes	Karl Diehl, Peterswaldau
ols	Union Ges. für Metallindustrie, Sils van de Loo, Auschwitz plant
ona	unknown
oss	unknown
oxo	Teuto-Metallwerke GmbH, Osnabrück
oyd	unknown
oyj	Atelier de Construction de Tarbes, France
p	Ruhrstahl, Brackwede
p	Polte Armaturen- u. Maschinenfabrik AG, Magdeburg, Saxony
pad	T. Bergmann & Co., Bernau plant, Berlin
pcd	T. Bergmann & Co., Bernau plant, Berlin
pjj	Haerens Ammunitionsarsenalet, Copenhagen, Denmark
pla	unknown
pmf	unknown
pmt	unknown
pmu	unknown
pvf	Optische Werke O. Reichert, Vienna
qa	William Prym, Stolberg, Rheinland
qlv	unknown
qnv	unknown
qrb	Pyrotechnische Fabrik, Bologna, Italy
qve	Karl Walther, Zella-Mehlis, Thuringia
r	Westfälische-Anhaltische Sprengstoff AG, Reinsdorf plant
ra	Deutsche Messingwerke, C. Eveking AG, Berlin-Niederschönweide
rde	unknown
rdf	unknown
rfo	unknown
rhs	unknown
rln	Karl Zeiss, Jena
rrk	unknown

rtl	unknown
s	Dynamit AG (formerly A. Nobel & Co.), Lumbrays plant
she	unknown
skd	Selve-Kornbiegel-Dornheim AG, Suhl plant
suk	unknown
sup	unknown
svw	Mauser-Werke, Oberndorf on the Neckar
swp	Waffenwerke Brünn AG, Brünn, Czechoslovakia
t	Dynamit AG, Troisdorf plant
ta	Dürener Metallwerke AG, Berlin-Borsigwalde
tjk	unknown
tka	unknown
tko	unknown
tpk	unknown
tpn	unknown
tvw	unknown
ua	Osnabrücker Kupfer- u. Drahtwerke AG, Osnabrück
unt	unknown
uxa	unknown
va	Kabel- u. Metallwerke Neumeyer AG, Nürnberg
vs	unknown
vso	unknown
vys	unknown
vzg	Vereinigte Zünder- u. Kabelwerke, Meissen
w	Gesellschaft zur Verwertung Chem. Erzeugnisse, Wolfratshausen plant
wa	Hasag, Hugo Schneider AG, Lampenfabrik, Leipzig
wc	Hasag, Hugo Schneider AG, Meuselwitz plant, Thuringia
wd	Hasag, Hugo Schneider AG, Taucha plant
we	Hasag, Hugo Schneider AG, Langewiesen plant
wf	Hasag, Hugo Schneider AG, Kielce plant, Poland
wg	Hasag, Hugo Schneider AG, Altenburg plant
wh	Hasag, Hugo Schneider AG, Eisenach plant
wj	Hasag, Hugo Schneider AG, Oberweissbach plant
wk	Hasag, Hugo Schneider AG, Schlieben plant
wn	Hasag, Hugo Schneider AG, Dernabach plant, Thuringia
wtf	unknown
x	unknown

xa	Busch & Jäger, Lüdenscheider Metallwerke, Lüdenscheid
y	Jagdpatronen, Zündhütchen- u- Metallwarenfabrik AG, Nagyteteny plant, Budapest
ya	Sächsische Metallwarenfabrik, August Wellner & Sohn, Aue, Saxony
zb	Kupferwerk Ilsenburg AG, Ilsenburg, Harz

NUMBER CODES

P 25	unknown
27	B. Geipel GmbH, Waffenfabrik Erma, Erfurt
P 28	Waffen- u. Munitionsfabrik, Karlsruhe plant
P 34	unknown
42	Mauser-Werke, Oberndorf on the Neckar
R 42	Mauser-Werke, Oberndorf on the Neckar
S 42	Mauser-Werke, Oberndorf on the Neckar
S 42G	Mauser-Werke, Oberndorf on the Neckar
S 67	H. Uttendorfer, Munitionsfabrik, Nürnberg
P 69	Selier & Bellot, Schönebeck on the Elbe
P 94	Kabel- & Metallwarenfabrik Neumeyer AG, Nürnberg
B 120	Dynamit AG, Empelde plant
122	Hugo Schmeisser
P 131	DWM-Werk, Borsigwalde
P 132	unknown
P 151	Rheinisch-Westfälische Sprengstoffwerke, Nürnberg-Stadeln
P 153	unknown
P 154	Polte, Lüneburg
P 162	unknown
P 163	unknown
P 181	Schneider AG, Altenburg
P 186	unknown
P 198	Metallwarenfabrik Treuenbritzen, Belsig, Mark
P 207	Metallwarenfabrik Odertal GmbH, Odertal
P 224	unknown
237	Mauser-Werke, Oberndorf on the Neckar
P 249	Finower Industrie GmbH, Finow
P 265	unknown
P 287	unknown

P 315	Marisches Walzwerk GmbH, Stramberg
P 316	Westfälische Metallindustrie, Lippstadt
P 327	unknown
P 334	Mansfeld AG, Rothenburg, Saale
P 340	Metallwarenfabrik Silberhütte, St. Andreasberg
P 345	unknown
P 346	H. Huck, Metallwarenfabrik, Nürnberg
P 369	unknown
P 370	unknown
P 379	Scharfenberg & Teubert, Breitungen
P 382	unknown
P 397	unknown
P 398	unknown
P 400	unknown
P 405	Dynamit AG, Durlach
P 413	unknown
P 414	unknown
P 416	unknown
P 417	unknown
P 442	unknown
P 457	unknown
480	Carl Walther, Zella-Mehlis
P 490	unknown
P 491	unknown
P 635	Munitionsfabrik Wöllersdorf, Vienna
660	Steyr-Daimler-Puch AG, Steyr, Austria
925	Mauser-Werke, Oberndorf on the Neckar
945	Waffenfabrik Brünn AG, Brno, Czechoslovakia

CPSIA information can be obtained at www.ICGtesting.com
Printed in the USA
BVOW071252140113

310451BV00001B/46/A